INTERNATIONAL DIFFERENCES
in the
LABOR MARKET
PERFORMANCE
of
IMMIGRANTS

George J. Borjas

University of California
Santa Barbara

1988

W. E. Upjohn Institute for Employment Research
Kalamazoo, Michigan

Library of Congress Cataloging-in-Publication Data

Borjas, George J.
 International differences in the labor market performance
 of immigrants.

 Bibliography: p.
 Includes index.
 1. Alien labor—United States. 2. Alien labor—Canada.
3. Alien labor—Australia. 4. Alien labor. 5. Emigration
and immigration. 6. Immigrants. I. Title.
HD8081.A5B66 1988   331.6'2   88-28017
ISBN 0-88099-065-1
ISBN 0-88099-064-3 (pbk.)

ii

iii

Author

George J. Borjas is a professor of economics at the University of California, Santa Barbara, and a research associate of the National Bureau of Economic Research. He received his Ph.D. from Columbia University and is co-editor of *Hispanics in the U.S. Economy* (1985).

Acknowledgements

This research has benefited from comments and suggestions made by many colleagues over a period of many years. I am particularly grateful to Gary Becker, Stephen Bronars, Richard Freeman, Daniel Hamermesh, and Frank Vella, whose reactions to this project and to related work influenced the direction of the research. This paper has also benefited from the comments of many seminar participants, particularly those at the National Bureau of Economic Research and the University of Chicago. I am also grateful to Robert Gregory and his colleagues at the Australian National University. I learned a great deal about the Australian immigration debate during my two-week stay at ANU in the spring of 1987. Finally, I am grateful to Bernt Bratsberg for exceptional research assistance.

Contents

1 Introduction 1

2 Immigration Policies in the Receiving Countries 9
    The United States 9
    Canada 12
    Australia 14

3 An Economic Model of Immigration 19

4 Empirical Framework 35

5 Data 41

6 1980–1981 Cross-Section Results 47

7 Cohort and Assimilation Effects 55

8 Determinants of Immigrant Sorting Across Host Countries 73

9 Labor Flows Between Canada and the United States 79

10 Summary and Conclusions 95

    Bibliography 99

    Index 103

Tables

1.1 Nativity Status of the Population in the Host Countries   1

1.2 Migration Flows to the U.S., Canada, and
Australia in 1959–1981   6

2.1 Migration Flows Into the United States, 1959–81   11

2.2 Percent of U.S. Immigrants Using a ''Family-Reunification''
Provision of the Law   12

2.3 Migration Flows Into Canada, 1959–81   14

2.4 Migration Flows Into Australia, 1959–81   16

5.1 Summary Statistics in Immigrant and Native Samples   43

6.1 1980/1981 Cross-Section Regressions in Host Countries   48

6.2 Earnings Differentials Between Immigrants and Natives
in 1980–81 Cross-Sections   51

7.1 Cohort Effects: Earnings of Immigrant Cohorts Relative
to the 1975–1980 Cohort   56

7.2 Decomposition of Quality Change Between 1960–64
and 1975–80 Cohorts in U.S. and Canada   60

7.3 Rates of Earnings Growth and Assimilation   62

7.4 Earnings Differentials Between Immigrants and Natives
at the Time of Entry   63

7.5 Present Value Differentials Between Immigrants and Natives   67

8.1 Determinants of Immigrant Quality Across Host Countries   75

9.1 Foreign-Born Populations in Canada and the United States   80

9.2 Aggregate Economic Indicators for U.S. and Canada   81

9.3 Summary Characteristics   82

9.4 Earnings Functions for Natives and Transnational Immigrants   85

9.5 Earnings Functions for Other Immigrants   87

9.6 Predicted Wage Differentials Between Immigrants
and Natives at Time of Migration   88

9.7   Average Rates of Growth in Immigrant and Native Earnings   90

9.8   Predicted Present Value Differentials Between
      Immigrants and Natives   91

Figures

7.1   Relative Wage of Immigrant Cohorts in the Host Countries   69

7.2(a)   Relative Wage of African Cohorts in the Host Countries   70

7.2(b)   Relative Wage of European Cohorts in the Host Countries   70

7.2(c)   Relative Wage of Asian Cohorts in the Host Countries   71

7.2(d)   Relative Wage of Latin American Cohorts
          in the Host Countries   71

1

Introduction

The migration of large flows of persons across national boundaries has been an important component of demographic change since Biblical times. International differences in economic and political conditions remain sufficiently strong to encourage the flows of millions of persons across countries. United Nations statistics, for example, show that nearly 5 million persons migrated to a different country in the 1975–1980 period.[1] The national origin of these persons exhibits a substantial variance: practically every country in the world contributes to the pool of persons who believe that better opportunities exist elsewhere *and* who are willing to incur the costs necessary to experience those opportunities. On the other hand, these peregrinators tend to migrate to only a handful of destination countries. In particular, about two-thirds of all immigrants in the 1975–1980 period migrated to one of three countries: Australia, Canada, and the United States.

Of course, each of these three countries is characterized by a long history of immigration. Table 1.1, for example, shows that the percentage of the population that is foreign-born in each of these three host countries has been large throughout the 20th century. In 1910, 14 percent of the U.S. population, 22 percent of the Canadian population, and 18 percent of the Australian population were foreign-born. By 1980 the U.S. share of foreign-born persons in the population had declined to 6.2 percent, the Canadian share had declined to 15.9 percent, and the Australian share had increased to 20.6 percent. Immigration still remains an important component of demographic change in these three "magnet" countries.[2]

The numerical (and economic) importance of the immigrant population in the labor markets in each of these host countries has renewed interest among economists in the old question of how immigrants do in

Table 1.1 Nativity Status of the Population in the Host Countries

Period	Percent of population foreign-born		
	USA	Canada	Australia
1910–11	14.4	22.0	17.6
1930–33	11.3	22.2	13.7
1950–54	6.6	14.4	14.3
1960–61	5.4	15.6	16.9
1970–71	4.7	15.2	20.2
1980–81	6.2	15.9	20.6
1980 Population (in millions)	226.5	24.3	14.6

SOURCES: Zubrzycki (1981, p. 161); 1981 Censuses of Australia and Canada; U.S. Department of Commerce (1986).

the labor market of the receiving country. Most of this research has focused on the American experience, although a few similar studies have also been conducted using Canadian or Australian census data.[3] This literature, for the most part, compares the earnings of immigrants to the earnings of natives in one of the host countries and makes inferences about the degree of adaptation or "assimilation" of the immigrant population in that country based on those comparisons.

The early studies in this literature used a single cross-section data set (such as the 1970 U.S. Census of Population) to compare immigrant earnings to the earnings of natives. These cross-sectional studies of immigrant earnings revealed two remarkable empirical findings: (1) the age/earnings profile of immigrants was significantly steeper than the age/earnings profile of "comparable" natives (i.e., natives with the same education and other socioeconomic characteristics as immigrants); and (2) although immigrant earnings were smaller than the earnings of comparable natives in the first few years after the migration took place, within 10–15 years the earnings of immigrants "caught up" and surpassed the earnings of comparable natives. Hence for a significant fraction of the working life cycle, immigrants earned substantially *more* than comparable natives.

The first of these findings was interpreted in the context of the human capital framework. Since the slope of an earnings profile (i.e., the rate at which earnings grow as the individual ages), *by assumption,* measures the extent to which such human capital investments as education, on-the-job training, etc., are taking place, the finding that immigrant earnings rose at a faster rate than native earnings must imply that immigrants invest more in human capital than natives. In fact, it seems quite plausible to argue that as immigrants learn the language and culture and gain information about the U.S. labor market and where the best-paying jobs are located, some "catching-up" of immigrant earnings to native earnings is inevitable.

The second of the empirical findings in cross-section studies (namely, that immigrant earnings "overtake" the earnings of comparable natives) is not entirely consistent with the human capital framework. There is, in theory, no reason why immigrants would want to accumulate *more* human capital than comparable natives. Hence the explanation of this empirical result lies in the hypothesis that immigrants must have brought with them a sizable amount of *unobserved* human capital (the human capital *must be* unobserved since earnings are being compared between immigrants and natives of the same education and socioeconomic characteristics). This explanation, in effect, assumes that immigrants are in some sense more driven and more motivated than natives, and hence it is not surprising that, given the chance, immigrants are more successful than natives in the U.S. labor market. The overtaking result is thus explained by assuming the existence of an unobserved ability differential between immigrants and natives. This ability differential may arise because immigrants are a nonrandom sample of the population from the countries of origin, and because the migration decision led to the self-selection of individuals who have a little more initiative, drive, and motivation than the average person in the population of the host country.

Recently, a "second-generation" phase of the literature has developed. These studies raise important questions and doubts about both the methodology used in the early cross-section analyses, and about the validity of the economic and selection assumptions used in explaining the results. The more recent studies begin with the observation that a single cross-section regression of earnings on age (or years-since-migration) confounds two important effects: the impact of pure aging on earnings growth, and the fact that different immigrant cohorts may differ substantially in productivity or quality. In other words, the observation that earnings and years-since-migration are strongly and positively correlated could be due to the fact that immigrants assimilate quickly, or to the fact that earlier immigrant waves are more productive than the more recent immigrant waves. Since regressions estimated in a single cross-section of data cannot separately identify aging and cohort effects, the recent literature analyzes the earnings of immigrants using either longitudinal data (Borjas 1987b; Jasso and Rosenzweig 1985) or using a series of cross-sections (such as the 1970 and 1980 U.S. Censuses) to "track" specific cohorts of immigrants over time (see Beggs and Chapman 1987; Bloom and Gunderson 1987; and Borjas 1985).

Although these studies use different data sets collected in different host countries, a single theme seems to be emerging from the recent literature: analyses of immigrant earnings that use a single cross-section of data provide a seriously flawed view of the assimilation process. For example, in contrast to findings of rapid earnings growth for the first-generation immigrant population, the "second-generation" studies find very small rates of earnings growth, so that immigrant "assimilation" is a relatively weak phenomenon in the labor market, and overtaking is almost never observed for the more recent immigrant waves. In addition, these studies find that different waves of immigrants (even from the same country of origin) differ significantly in their earnings capacities. Borjas (1985), for example, documents that the more recent waves of immigrants arriving in the United States have significantly lower earnings capacities than the waves of immigrants who arrived 10 or 20 years earlier. These various findings thus suggest that the typical cross-section correlation between immigrant earnings and years-since-migration is mainly attributable to the fact the cohort effects are important, and not to the existence of strong assimilation rates in the first-generation, foreign-born population.

Despite the recent substantive advances in the literature, these studies (like the first-generation studies that preceded them) implicitly present an extremely myopic view of the immigration experience. Due to the construction of the available data sets, all that seems to matter in this literature is the comparison of immigrant earnings in the country of destination with the earnings of natives in that country. This myopic view ignores the fact that persons emigrating any country of origin usually have more than one potential country of destination. In a sense, potential migrants enter an "immigration market" where different host countries reveal the costs and benefits of emigrating to each particular country, and individuals then make a decision whether to emigrate or not, and which country to migrate to, based on these comparisons. The analysis presented in this monograph incorporates the idea of an "immigration market" by focusing on a comparative study of the labor market performance of immigrants in each of the three main host countries in the postwar period, Australia, Canada, and the United States. The existence of an immigration market suggests that the distribution of foreign-born persons across these three countries is not random. This nonrandom sorting raises important questions about the kinds of self-selection biases that are generated by the endogenous migration decision of individuals.

The size of the flows generated by the self-selection of migrants into each of the three potential countries of destination is documented in table 1.2. Over the 1959–1981 period, over 14.7 million persons left the various countries of origin and migrated to Australia, Canada, or the United States. Sixty-one percent of these migrants chose the United States as their destination, and the remainder were split between Australia and Canada. Table 1.2 also shows, however, that these statistics vary significantly between the early part of the period (1959–1970) and the later part of the period (1971–1981). Recent migrants are disproportionately more likely to select the U.S. as their destination (nearly two-thirds of migrants in the 1970s did so), and disproportionately less likely to choose Australia as their destination (only 14 percent did so).

Table 1.2 also shows that these aggregate statistics mask important country-of-origin differences. During the 1971–1981 period, the United States was less likely to receive immigrants from Africa, the United Kingdom, Europe and Oceania, and significantly more likely to receive immigrants from Asia and North and South America. Canada, on the other hand, seemed a relatively attractive destination for

Table 1.2   Migration Flows to the U.S., Canada, and Australia in 1959–1981

| | 1959–70 | | | |
Origin	Number (1000s)	% to U.S.	% to Canada	% to Australia
Africa	115.1	37.5	29.6	32.8
America	2111.6	84.9	13.4	1.7
Asia	708.3	69.5	19.2	11.3
U.K.	1322.9	20.3	28.8	50.9
Europe (Excl. U.K.)	2583.4	47.5	28.9	23.6
Oceania	123.7	18.9	32.5	48.6
Total	6965.0	55.2	23.3	21.5
	1971–81			
Origin	Number (1000s)	% to U.S.	% to Canada	% to Australia
Africa	220.5	48.3	32.4	19.3
America	2687.7	81.0	15.9	3.1
Asia	2580.8	73.5	17.7	8.7
U.K	751.1	18.4	31.7	49.9
Europe (Excl. U.K.)	1309.2	55.7	26.0	18.3
Oceania	176.9	23.5	19.4	57.2
Total	7726.2	65.9	20.3	13.8
	1959–81			
Origin	Number (1000s)	% to U.S.	% to Canada	% to Australia
Africa	335.5	44.6	31.5	23.9
America	4799.3	82.7	14.8	2.5
Asia	3289.0	72.7	18.0	9.3
U.K.	2074.0	19.6	29.8	50.5
Europe (Excl. U.K.)	3892.6	50.3	27.9	21.8
Oceania	300.5	21.6	24.8	53.6
Total	14690.9	60.8	21.7	17.5

SOURCES: U.S. Department of Commerce (various issues), U.S. Immigration and Naturalization Service (various issues), *Historical Statistics of Canada, Canada Yearbook* (various issues), *Australian Immigration*.

immigrants from Africa, the United Kingdom and Europe, and Australia was also a preferred destination for persons leaving the United Kingdom. Nearly half of the 2 million persons who left the U.K. in the 1959–1981 period migrated to Australia.

This monograph presents an empirical analysis of the labor market performance of the foreign-born population in each of these three countries of destination. Its main objective is to ascertain the impact of the endogenous migration decision on the quality of the immigrant flows reaching each of the countries. The analysis will be guided by two important conceptual tools: the existence of an immigration market and the hypothesis that individuals are wealth-maximizers. These two tools suggest that individuals enter an immigration market where various countries give ''wage offers'' to potential migrants, and that individuals then migrate to or stay in the country that has the highest wage offer (net of migration costs). It will be seen that this conceptual framework provides a very useful method for analyzing the nonrandom nature of the sorting of immigrants across host countries.

The empirical analysis below provides a joint study of five censuses conducted in the three host countries since 1970: the 1970 and 1980 U.S. Censuses, the 1971 and 1981 Canadian Censuses, and the 1981 Australia Census. It will be seen that the systematic study of international differences in the relative performance of immigrants in the labor market provides substantive insight into the self-selection process that determines the composition of the pool of migrants. In addition, the empirical analysis illustrates the importance of changes in immigration policy in determining both the national origin and skill composition of the migrant flow reaching a particular country of destination.

NOTES

[1]These statistics are obtained from United Nations (1982, p. 44). The calculations discussed in the text ignore the large (and presumably temporary) population flows from Ethiopia to Somalia in the late 1970s, as well as the movement of guest workers to oil producing countries in the Middle East.

[2]See Borjas and Tienda (1987) for a discussion of the contribution of immigration to demographic change in the United States. A broader, historical account of the role

played by international migration flows in demographic change is given by Zolberg (1983).

[3]The studies include Borjas (1982), Carliner (1980), Chiswick (1978, 1987), Chiswick and Miller (1985), DeFreitas (1980), Long (1980) and Tandon (1978). The literature was recently surveyed by Greenwood and McDowell (1986).

2

Immigration Policies
in the Receiving Countries

The migration decision is guided by comparisons of income streams across countries *given* the institutional constraints that permit the migration flows to occur. The fact that all countries restrict the number and the types of persons who can cross their boundaries imposes severe restrictions on the mobility of potential migrants. Different migration policies provide different incentive structures and thus lead to a different pool of migrants. It is, therefore, instructive to begin the analysis with a detailed discussion of immigration policies in each of the three countries of destination considered in this monograph.[1]

The United States

Prior to the 1965 Amendments to the Immigration and Nationality Act, immigration to the United States was regulated by a system of numerical quotas allocating the limited number of potential visas among countries in the Eastern Hemisphere. The numerical limits for each country were established on the basis of the ethnic composition of the U.S. population in 1920. Hence they led to significant restrictions on migration from Asian and African countries and favored immigration from European countries. In 1964, for example, European countries were allocated a total of 158,161 visas, while Asian and African countries typically received 100 visas per country.[2]

The pre-1965 statutes also established a preference system regulating the allocation of the limited number of visas available for countries in the Eastern Hemisphere among the many applicants. In general, this preference system favored applicants with occupations or skills "urgently needed'' in the United States: at least half of all quota visas were reserved for such individuals and their families. The remaining visas were then allocated on the basis of kinship relationships between the potential migrants and persons residing in the United States.

In the pre-1965 period, immigration from Western Hemisphere countries was not numerically limited under the law, but potential migrants had to satisfy the usual health, criminal, political, and self-sufficiency background requirements. The mechanism by which entry visas were granted to Western Hemisphere applicants was not specified in the pre-1965 Immigration and Nationality Act. It is, therefore, likely that administrative decisions and consular officials played a particularly influential role in determining the size and the composition of the migrant pool from North and South American countries during this period.

The 1965 Amendments (and subsequent changes in the immigration law through the early 1980s) responded to the charges that the preference system discriminated on the basis of national origin by disposing of the country-specific numerical quotas. Instead, an annual limit of 20,000 visas per country was instituted, subject to a worldwide limit of 290,000 immigrants (which in the late 1970s was composed of a 170,000 limit for immigrants from the Eastern Hemisphere and a 120,000 limit for immigrants from the Western Hemisphere).

The 1965 Amendments also institutionalized the concept of ''family reunification'' as a central goal of U.S. immigration policy. Two provisions in the law achieve this objective. First, close relatives of adult U.S. citizens (parents, spouses, and children) can enter the United States *without* having to qualify under the numerical restrictions specified in the Amendments. In fact, nearly 30 percent of all migrants in the 1980s qualified under this provision of the law (U.S. Department of Commerce 1986).[3] In addition, the preference system was revised so that at least 80 percent of the 290,000 numerically restricted visas were given to persons who were more distant relatives of U.S. citizens or residents. Hence the 1965 Amendments led to a fundamental de-emphasis of occupational and skill requirements in the screens used to determine the immigrant pool. By the 1980s, the combined impact of these two provisions in the 1965 Amendments was responsible for

Table 2.1 Migration Flows Into the United States, 1959–81

Origin	Period of migration					
	1959–70		1971–81		1959–81	
	No. (in 1000s)	% of total	No. (in 1000s)	% of total	No. (in 1000s)	% of total
Africa	43.2	1.1	106.5	2.0	149.7	1.7
America	1792.0	46.6	2175.7	42.7	3967.7	44.3
Asia	492.2	12.8	1898.1	37.2	2390.3	26.7
U.K.	268.8	7.0	138.5	2.7	407.3	4.6
Europe (Excl. U.K.)	1228.2	31.9	729.5	14.3	1957.7	21.9
Oceania & other	23.4	.6	41.5	.8	64.9	.7
Total	3847.8		5089.9		8937.7	

SOURCE: U.S. Department of Commerce (various issues), U.S. Immigration and Naturalization Services (various issues).

the fact that over 70 percent of all immigration to the United States occurred under one of the two kinship provisions in the law (U.S. Department of Commerce 1986).

The redistribution of quotas across hemispheres and countries initiated by the 1965 Amendments also led to a substantial change in the national origin composition of the foreign-born population in the United States. Table 2.1 illustrates the extent of these changes. During the 1959–1970 period, nearly one-third of all immigrants originated in European countries, and only 13 percent of the immigrants were of Asian descent. In the subsequent decade, the fraction of immigrants originating in Europe had declined to 14.3 percent, while the fraction originating in Asia had nearly tripled to 37.2 percent. It is of interest to note that the fraction of immigrants originating in the Western Hemisphere did not change much across the two decades (46.6 percent in the 1960s and 42.7 percent in the 1970s). This is probably due to the fact that the 1965 Amendments, for the first time, imposed numerical restrictions on the number of North and South American immigrants who could *legally* enter the United States.

The second significant impact of the 1965 Amendments was the

Table 2.2   Percent of U.S. Immigrants Using a "Family-Reunification" Provision of the Law

Origin	1965	1970	1975	1980
Asia[a]	76.3	58.8	67.9	69.4
Africa[a]	20.6	28.0	49.9	75.7
Europe	26.6	69.2	73.2	69.0
Western Hemisphere[b]	—	—	—	79.0

SOURCE: U.S. Immigration and Naturalization Service (various issues).

a. The statistics presented for these continents for fiscal year 1965 are somewhat unreliable because of the small numbers of immigrants originating in these continents prior to the 1965 Amendments.

b. These statistics cannot be calculated prior to 1977–78.

de-emphasis on occupational and skill characteristics in determining the probability of entry into the United States. Table 2.2 presents the fraction of immigrants, by continent of origin, that entered the United States by using a family reunification provision of the law. During the early 1960s, for example, only about a quarter of the immigrants originating in Europe entered the U.S. under these provisions. By 1980, however, the fraction had increased to 69.0 percent. Similarly, one of the first numerically sizable waves of Asian immigrants (the 1970 cohort) to enter the United States after the restrictions had been lifted was composed of 58.8 percent "family migrants." This share increased to 69.4 percent by 1980.

Canada

Canadian immigration policy, until 1962, also had a preferential treatment of immigrants originating in Western European countries. The 1962 Immigration Act (and further relatively minor changes in regulations and the statutes through the 1970s) removed the country-of-origin and racial restrictions, and shifted emphasis towards skills requirements. Under the new regulations, immigrants were essentially grouped into three categories: (1) sponsored immigrants (which included close relatives of Canadian residents or citizens); (2) nominated relatives (which included more distant relatives of Canadian residents or citizens); and (3) independent migrants. Applicants for visas in the last two of these categories were screened by means of a point system: potential migrants were graded and given up to 100 points. Points were awarded according to the applicant's education (a point per year of schooling, up to 20 points), occupational demand (up to 10 points if the applicant's occupation was in strong demand in Canada), age (up to 10 points for applicants under the age of 35, minus 1 point for each year over age 35), arranged employment (10 points if the applicant had a job offer from a Canadian employer), a personal "assessment" by the immigration officer based on the applicant's motivation and initiative (up to 15 points), etc. Generally, an applicant needed to obtain 50 points out of the 100 total points in order to receive permission to migrate into Canada.

Canada also regulated the total number of persons who could be granted entry into Canada in any given year. The available number of slots, unlike that of the United States, was not determined by statute. Instead it was announced annually by the Minister of Employment and Immigration after a review of economic and political conditions in Canada. During the late 1970s, the annual limit on the number of immigrants was roughly 100,000.

⌈In 1976, the Immigration Act was amended to incorporate the goal of family reunification as an important objective of Canadian immigration policy. Since the provisions in this Act did not go into effect until 1978, the impact of these changes on migration prior to the 1981 Census (the most recent Canadian data set to be analyzed below) is likely to be minimal. Nevertheless, it is of interest to note that the fraction of migrants who belonged to the category of "independent migrants" had been declining even prior to the 1976 Amendments.⌉ During the 1960s, for example, 60–64 percent of all immigrants were "independent," while during the 1974–76 period the fraction had declined to 51–55 percent (Kubat 1979, p. 31). Hence even without an explicit change in the law, the Canadian experience regarding family reunification bears a slight resemblance to the more abrupt changes experienced by the United States.

In addition, as Table 2.3 shows, the national origin of the Canadian

Table 2.3   Migration Flows Into Canada, 1959–81

| | Period of migration | | | | | |
| | 1959–70 | | 1971–81 | | 1959–81 | |
Origin	No. (in 1000s)	% of Total	No. (in 1000s)	% of Total	No. (in 1000s)	% of Total
Africa	34.1	2.1	71.5	4.6	105.6	3.3
America	283.5	17.5	427.9	27.3	711.4	22.3
Asia	136.3	8.4	457.3	29.1	593.6	18.6
U.K.	381.2	23.5	237.8	15.2	619.0	19.4
Europe (Excl. U.K.)	745.4	46.0	340.1	21.7	1085.5	34.0
Oceania & other	40.2	2.5	34.3	2.2	74.5	2.3
Total	1620.7		1568.9		3189.6	

SOURCE: *Historical Statistics of Canada,* Canada Yearbook (various issues).

immigrant population also changed drastically in the post-1959 period. For example, 23.5 percent of immigrants in the 1960s originated in the U.K., and an additional 46.0 percent originated in other European countries. During the 1970s, the percentages declined to 15.2 and 21.7, respectively. Conversely, the fraction of immigrants originating in Asia was only 8.4 percent during the 1960s, and more than tripled to 29.1 percent during the 1970s. Hence the national origin composition of migrants choosing Canada as a destination changed as much as a result of the 1962 Canadian Immigration Act as the national origin composition of migrants choosing the United States changed as a result of the 1965 Amendments.

Australia

Australian immigration policy has a long history of restricting the migration of persons who are not of British origin. Prior to World War II, immigration policy in Australia almost exclusively emphasized the recruitment of migrants from Great Britain. Further, to compete with the other possible countries of destination available to potential British migrants, the Australian government assisted the migrant by incurring part of the migration and resettlement costs. The assistance program was substantial: of the 2.5 million settlers that migrated to Australia between 1788 and 1939, nearly half did so with government assistance.

The restrictions against migration from countries other than the U.K. or Northern and/or Western Europe became known as the "White Australia Policy." These restrictions were not, for the most part, statutory, but instead operated through the power of administrators to accept or reject potential applicants without justifying their decisions. In addition, financial assistance to cover transportation and resettlement costs was rarely granted to Asians and other "nondesirable" migrant groups. The net effect of the White Australia Policy, therefore, was that non-Europeans could enter Australia only for business or educational reasons.

World War II raised doubts about the ability of the small Australian population to defend the continent, and the government instituted a national policy to increase population by about 2 percent per year, with half of the increase to be accomplished through immigration. Initially, the government strictly adhered to the principles of the White Australia Policy: the objective was for the migrants to be over 90 percent British. Price (1979), for example, reports that the Australian government even refused to let Australian soldiers bring back their Japanese wives after the war.

The objective of recruiting large numbers of British migrants to increase the postwar Australian population, however, could not be attained. As a result, Australia signed formal arrangements with a number of European countries (such as Germany, the Netherlands, Malta, Italy, and Greece) to recruit and assist persons from these countries in their migration to Australia. These migrants, however, were generally not given the same level of financial assistance as British migrants. It was only in the early 1970s that equality in the assistance of transportation costs and settlement benefits was reached.

Internal political changes in Australia led to the formal abolishment of the White Australia Policy in 1972. An immigration policy devoid of discrimination by national origin and race was instituted. This

Table 2.4   Migration Flows Into Australia, 1959–81

| | Period of migration | | | | | |
| | 1959–70 | | 1971–81 | | 1959–81 | |
Origin	No. (in 1000s)	% of Total	No. (in 1000s)	% of Total	No. (in 1000s)	% of Total
Africa	37.8	2.5	42.5	4.0	80.2	3.1
America	36.1	2.4	84.1	7.9	120.2	4.7
Asia	79.8	5.3	225.4	21.1	305.1	11.9
U.K.	672.9	44.9	374.8	35.1	1047.7	40.9
Europe (Excl. U.K.)	609.8	40.8	239.6	22.4	849.4	33.1
Oceania & other	60.1	4.0	101.1	9.5	161.1	6.3
Total	1496.3		1067.5		2563.7	

SOURCE: *Australian Immigration* 1978.

immigration policy introduced a point system, similar to that used by Canada, that stressed educational background and occupational skills. Also, as in Canada, the total number of immigrants admitted in any given year is not statutorily determined, but can be changed rapidly due to economic or political factors. During the early 1980s, Australia began to stress the concept of family reunification in its migration policy (see Birrell 1983). This recent shift in Australian immigration policy, however, will not have any impact on the 1981 Australian Census data that will be analyzed below.

The impact of these changes in immigration policy on the composition of the immigrant pool reaching Australia can be seen in table 2.4. Although the U.K. accounted for nearly half of the migrants in the 1960s, it only accounted for about a third of the migrants during the 1970s. A similar decline is observed in the fraction of immigrants originating in other European countries: from 40.8 percent to 22.4 percent. On the other hand, the fraction of immigrants originating in Asia increased from 5.3 to 21.1 percent, a fourfold increase in a 10-year period. Changes in the national origin composition of the migrant flow into Australia, therefore, closely resemble the changes in the migrant flows choosing Canada and the United States.

NOTES

[1]This section is heavily influenced by the excellent descriptions and summaries of immigration policies given by Boyd (1976), Keely (1979), Keely and Elwell (1981), Kubat (1979), and Price (1979).

[2]See U.S. Immigration and Naturalization Service (1965).

[3]See Jasso and Rosenzweig (1986) for an analysis of the ''multiplier effect'' in the kinship provisions of the immigration law.

3

An Economic Model
of Immigration

The differences in immigration policies documented in the previous section, alongside the differences in economic conditions among potential host countries, suggest that potential emigrants from a given country of origin face different "compensation packages" in each of the possible countries of destination. In effect, these differences in immigration policies and economic conditions create an "immigration market," wherein the various host countries compete for the available pool of immigrants. The sorting of immigrants across competing host countries implies that in any given host country the foreign-born population is, in a sense, *doubly* self-selected. First, only a nonrandom sample of persons decide to emigrate any specific country of origin. Second, from this subset of persons, an even smaller nonrandom subset chooses a particular country as destination. The characteristics of the typical emigrant, therefore, are likely to differ significantly from the characteristics of the typical person in the country of origin who decided not to migrate. In addition, the characteristics of foreign-born persons are likely to differ substantially across countries of destination.

The economic model that explains the nature of this nonrandom sorting of immigrants and countries is formally identical to the study of occupational choice presented by Roy (1951). After all, the process of individuals choosing an occupation as they enter the labor market is similar to the process of individuals choosing a country of destination after entering the immigration market.

Suppose there are two countries, and migration flows from country 0 (the country of origin) to country 1 (the country of destination). This simple two-country framework ignores three potential complications. First, it is likely that persons born in country 1 consider the possibility of migrating to other countries, such as country 0. Unfortunately, data on emigration, particularly from the United States, is very scarce, and little can be done empirically about this problem. Second, even migrants choosing country 1 as the destination may find that things did not work out after migration took place (or perhaps worked out much better than expected). These unanticipated events may create incentives for return migration to country 0. Again, little is known, particularly in the United States, about the extent of return migration, and this problem is also ignored in what follows. Finally, individuals contemplating emigration from country 0, in fact, can "choose" from a number of potential countries of destination in the immigration market. There are two reasons why focusing on a two-country model is instructive. First, the basic insights provided by the economic theory of immigration are best grasped in a two-country framework. Second, as in most theories of international trade, generalization to n countries is conceptually simple, but technically quite difficult. The analysis below will utilize the simpler two-country setup for deriving the basic implications of the theory, and will discuss how these results apply in a more general model.[1]

Residents of the home country face an earnings distribution given by:

$$\ln \omega_0 = X \delta_0 + \epsilon_0, \tag{1}$$

where ω_0 gives the earnings of persons in the country of origin, and X is a vector of socioeconomic characteristics such as education, age, etc. These observed characteristics are "rewarded" at rate δ_0 in the country of origin. The random disturbance ϵ_0 is assumed to be independent of X, and to be normally distributed with mean zero and variance σ_0^2.

It is useful in what follows to interpret ϵ_0 as the component of earnings associated with "ability" or "luck" among individuals of similar socioeconomic characteristics. It should be noted that the assumption that ϵ_0 is normally distributed, although standard in the literature, is quite applicable for the problem at hand. Since the logarithm of earnings is assumed to be normal, earnings will be log-normal and positively skewed (i.e., a long tail to the right of the earnings distribution). The assumed shape of the earnings distribution, therefore, is quite close to the actual shape of earnings distributions found in data for many countries (Lydall, 1968).

The earnings distribution facing individuals in the labor market of the host country is given by:[2]

$$\ln \omega_1 = X\delta_1 + \epsilon_1. \tag{2}$$

The vector of coefficients δ_1 gives the value that the country of destination attaches to the socioeconomic characteristics X. The disturbance ϵ_1 is again assumed to be independent of X and is normally distributed with mean zero and variance σ_1^2.

The random variables ϵ_0 and ϵ_1 have correlation coefficient ρ. If ρ is positive and near unity, the economies of the host country and the country of destination value unobserved ability in the same way, while if ρ is negative, persons who do well in the country of origin possess unobserved characteristics that are not valued by the labor market of the country of destination. It is reasonable to suppose that for most pairs of countries of origin and destination, the correlation coefficient ρ is likely to be positive and sizable.

Equations (1) and (2) completely describe the earnings opportunities facing all individuals in both the country of origin and the country of destination. The main behavioral assumption of the analysis is that individuals born in country 0 compare the earnings streams in each of the two countries and decide to reside in the country where they get the highest earnings opportunities, net of migration costs. Three questions are raised by this simple framework. First, what factors determine the size of the migration flow generated by the income-maximization hypothesis? Second, what types of selection in the unobserved characteristics ϵ are created by the endogenous migration decision? In other words, is the nonrandom sample of migrants characterized by high or low levels of ability or "luck"? Third, what types of selection in the observed characteristics X are created by the endogenous migration decision? Are the migrants characterized by high or low levels of education and other observable socioeconomic characteristics?

Let C be the level of costs associated with migrating from country

0 to country 1. The income-maximization hypothesis implies that an individual will compare the available income stream in the country of origin (ω_0) with the net income available in country 1 ($\omega_1 - C$), and will reside in the country where the best income opportunities exist. This behavioral assumption can be written mathematically by defining an index variable, I, as:

$$I = (\omega_1 - C) - \omega_0. \tag{3}$$

Migration then occurs when the index variable I is positive, and the individual chooses to remain in the country of origin when the index variable I is negative. It is important to note that this framework essentially ignores the distinction between ''economic'' and ''noneconomic'' migrants, which is usually stressed in the migration literature. In this income-maximizing framework, all migration is ''economic'' in the sense that migration occurs when individuals profit from it. It will be seen below that the usual discussion of ''noneconomic'' migration (such as that associated with refugee flows across countries) can be easily understood within the income-maximizing framework.

Since individuals migrate from country 0 to country 1 when $I > 0$, the model can be easily seen to generate important empirical predictions as to which factors influence the size of the migration flow. These insights summarize the rather obvious economic content of the theory of migration proposed by Hicks (1966) and further elaborated by Sjaastad (1962). In particular, emigration from country 0 is more likely to occur the lower the mean level of income in country 0; migration from country 0 to country 1 is more likely to occur the higher the income levels are in country 1; and migration flows will be smaller the larger the level of mobility costs associated with moving from country 0 to country 1. Much of the literature on the internal migration of persons in the United States (i.e., movements across regions of the U.S.) is devoted to testing these theoretical predictions (see, for example, the survey by Greenwood 1975).

The immigration literature, on the other hand, has not historically been concerned with explaining the *size* of the migration flows. Instead, this literature has been interested in explaining the ''quality'' or composition of the migrant flow. As far back as 1919, for example, Paul H. Douglas was asking whether or not the skill composition of immigrant cohorts was constant across successive immigrant waves. The theory of migration presented in this monograph has important implications for such questions. In particular, the theory gives strong predictions about the kinds of people, both in terms of observed and unobserved characteristics, who choose to cross international boundaries and select a new country for a residence. Consider initially the selection mechanism in the unobserved characteristics ϵ. It is of substantial policy importance to determine whether the migrant flow is composed of high-ability persons (i.e., high values of ϵ) or of low-ability persons (i.e., low values of ϵ).

This problem can be addressed by considering the conditional expectations $E(\ln \omega_0 \mid X, I > 0)$ and $E(\ln \omega_1 \mid X, I > 0)$. The first of these terms gives the average earnings *in the country of origin* of persons who decided to emigrate that country, while the second of these terms gives the average earnings *in the country of destination* of persons who migrated from country 0. Note that these conditional means "hold constant" the vector of socioeconomic variables X. These conditional expectations are, therefore, useful in understanding how immigrant earnings vary from the earnings of other groups holding constant the observable characteristics X. These types of standardized differences measure the extent to which unobserved factors (such as ability) create wage differences among the various groups under analysis. Given the normality assumptions, these conditional means are given by:[3]

$$E(\ln \omega_0 \mid X, I > 0) = X\delta_0 + (\rho - \frac{\sigma_0}{\sigma_1})\,\lambda, \qquad (4)$$

$$E(\ln \omega_1 \mid X, I > 0) = X\delta_1 + (\frac{\sigma_1}{\sigma_0} - \rho)\,\lambda, \qquad (5)$$

where λ is a positive number. Note that the first terms in equations (4) and (5) give the means of the income distributions in the country of origin and in country of destination (for persons with characteristics

X). The second terms in equations (4) and (5) measure the extent to which the earnings of migrants differ from the means of the income distributions and are called the "selectivity biases" (Heckman 1979). These selectivity biases measure the extent to which the nonrandom composition of the immigrant pool in terms of unobserved characteristics or ability affects the earnings of migrants both in the country of origin and the country of destination.

Let Q_0 be the second term in equation (4), a measure of the wage differential between the average person born in country 0 and the average person that emigrated country 0. Let Q_1 be the second term in equation (5), a measure of the wage differential between the average person born in country 1 and the average immigrant in country 1. The variable Q_0 and Q_1 measure the "quality" of the migrant flow from country 0 to country 1 in terms of the unobserved characteristics of the migrant pool. If the person of average ability in the country of origin migrated to the host country, then $Q_0 = 0$. If, in addition, this migrant has ability equal to that of natives in the host country, then $Q_1 = 0$. Nonzero values of Q_0 or Q_1, therefore, indicate the extent to which the self-selection of the immigrant pool leads to a foreign-born population that is "nonaverage" in the host country. The model suggests three cases of substantive interest.

Positive Selection: $Q_0 > 0$ and $Q_1 > 0$.

This type of selection exists when migrants have above average earnings in the country of origin (given their characteristics X), and also have earnings in the host country which exceed the earnings of comparable natives. Inspection of equations (4) and (5) implies that the necessary and sufficient conditions for this type of selection to occur are:

$$\rho > \bar{\kappa} \text{ and } \sigma_1 > \sigma_0. \qquad (6)$$

where $\bar{\kappa}$ is a positive constant.[4]

If the correlation coefficient in the earnings across the two countries

ρ is sufficiently high *and* if income is more dispersed in the host country than in the country of origin, immigrants arriving in the host country will be selected from the upper tail of the home country's income distribution, and will outperform natives upon arrival to the host country. Intuitively, this occurs because the home country, in a sense, is "taxing" high-ability workers and "insuring" low-ability workers against poor labor market outcomes. These taxes and subsidies are, of course, reflected in the fact that the host country's income distribution has more inequality than the home country's income distribution. Since high-income workers benefit relatively more than low-income workers from migration to the host country (regardless of how much higher mean incomes in the home country may be relative to the country of origin) a "brain drain" is generated. The host country, with its greater degree of inequality in earnings opportunities, becomes a magnet for persons who are likely to do well in the labor market.

Negative Selection: $Q_0 < 0$ and $Q_1 < 0$.

This type of selection is generated when the host country draws persons who have below-average incomes in the country of origin, and who, holding characteristics constant, perform poorly in the host country's labor market. The necessary and sufficient conditions for negative selection to occur are:

$$\rho > \bar{\kappa} \text{ and } \sigma_1 < \sigma_0. \tag{7}$$

Negative selection again requires that the correlation in earnings across the two countries ρ be "sufficiently positive," but that the income distribution in the country of origin be more unequal than that in the host country. Intuitively, negative selection is generated when the host country "taxes" high-income workers relatively more than the country of origin, and provides better "insurance" for low-income workers against poor labor market outcomes. This opportunity set creates large incentives for low-ability persons to migrate, since they can improve their situation in the host country, and decreased incentives for high-ability persons to migrate, since income opportunities in the home country are more profitable.

Refugee Sorting: $Q_0 < 0$ and $Q_1 > 0$.

This kind of selection occurs when the host country draws below-average immigrants (in terms of the country of origin), but migrants perform quite well in the host country's labor market. The necessary and sufficient condition for this type of selection to occur is:

$$\rho < \bar{\kappa}. \tag{8}$$

In other words, if the correlation coefficient in earnings across the two countries ρ is negative or small, the composition of the migrant pool is likely to resemble a refugee population. For instance, it is likely that ρ is negative for countries that have recently experienced a communist takeover. After all, the change from a market economy to a communist system is often accompanied by structural changes in the income distribution, and by confiscation of entrepreneurial assets and redistribution to other persons. In essence, the income distribution of the country of origin becomes a mirror image of the prerevolution income distribution: Persons who did well prior to the political upheavals see their assets vanish and be given to persons who were not able to perform well in a market economy. The theoretical framework thus predicts that immigrants from such systems will be in the lower tail of the revolutionary income distribution, but will outperform the average worker in the host country, since the immigrant has characteristics that match very well with market economy conditions.

This simple economic model, therefore, provides a useful categorization of the factors that determine the quality or composition (in terms of unobserved characteristics) of the migrant pool. Several important implications of the model give some insight into a number of empirical findings in the literature. For example, many studies have documented the fact that refugee populations perform quite well in the U.S. labor market when compared to native workers of similar socioeconomic characteristics. These empirical results are consistent with the income-maximization hypothesis: Refugee populations, prior to the political changes which led to a worsening of their economic status, were relatively well-off in their country of origin. As noted earlier, there is no reason to resort to the arbitrary distinctions between "economic" and "noneconomic" migration to explain the refugee experience.

The theoretical framework presented here also provides an interesting explanation for the empirical finding that the quality of migrants to the United States has declined in the postwar period (where quality is defined as the wage differential between migrants and natives of the same measured skills). As noted earlier, prior to the 1965 Amendments to the Immigration and Nationality Act, immigration to the United States was regulated by numerical quotas. These quotas were based on the ethnic population of the United States in 1920 and thus encouraged immigration from Western European countries and restricted migration from other continents, particularly Asia. The favored countries have one important characteristic: their income distributions are probably much less dispersed than those of countries in Latin America or Asia. The 1965 Amendments abolished the discriminatory restrictions against immigration from non-European countries, established a numerical limit of 20,000 for legal migrants from any single country, and led to a substantial increase in the number of migrants originating in Asia and Latin America. The new flow of migrants thus originates in countries that are much more likely to have greater income inequality than the United States, and it would not be surprising, given the insights provided by the economic model of immigration, to find that the standardized earnings of immigrants declined as a result of the 1965 Amendments.

In addition, the 1965 Amendments led to a fundamental shift in the mechanism by which visas were allocated among potential migrants: the role played by observable skills and occupational characteristics was de-emphasized, and most visas began to be allocated according to the types of kinship relationships existing between potential migrants and persons currently residing in the United States. The economic model of immigration also suggests that this change in the statutes will lead to a substantial decline in immigrant quality. In particular, the family of the migrant that resides in the United States provides a "safety net" that insures the immigrant against poor labor market outcomes and unemployment periods in the months after migration. Low-ability persons who could not migrate without family connections to the United States, and hence without that insurance, will now find it worthwhile to do so. In effect, the kinship regulations in the immigration law create a lower bound in the income levels that low-skilled immigrants can attain in the United States, and hence make it more likely that immigrants are negatively selected from the population.

The discussion, therefore, shows that *both* immigration policies and economic conditions of host and origin countries can have a major impact on the size and composition of the migrant flow across countries. The model can thus be used to determine how the composition of the migrant flow will vary as a result of changes in these "exogenous" variables. This type of analysis has been formally conducted in my earlier studies (Borjas 1987a, 1987b) and can be succinctly summarized as follows.

1. An increase in the variance of the income distribution in the home country leads to a decrease in the quality of migrants reaching any country of destination. In other words, migrants originating in countries with larger levels of income inequality, holding constant the characteristics of the host country, are more likely to be negatively selected, and are therefore likely to have lower earnings than other migrant flows.

2. An increase in the variance of the income distribution in the country of destination leads to an increase in the quality of migrants choosing to migrate there. The greater the opportunities available to persons in a given host country, the more likely the migrant flow will be positively selected, and the greater the earnings of that migrant flow upon immigration.

3. Immigration policies that stress family reunification are likely to generate a migrant flow that has lower earnings capacities than immigration policies stressing skills and occupational characteristics. This result arises because relatives in the host country "protect" the

immigrant from relatively poor labor market outcomes, and thus create migration incentives for persons who would not have migrated otherwise.

Up to this point, the study has focused on analyzing how the average *unobserved* ability-level of the migrant flow is determined by economic and political characteristics and by the immigration policies of the various countries participating in the immigration market. It is of interest to also analyze the factors that determine the composition of the migrant flow on the basis of observed skill characteristics, such as education.

The earnings functions in equations (1) and (2), alongside the hypothesis that individuals choose a country of residence according to the principle of income-maximization, provide an important insight. The migration of persons with larger levels of X is more likely if X has a higher return in the host country than in the country of origin, and the migration of persons with lower levels of X is more likely if the country of origin values the characteristic X more than the host country. An understanding of this result can be gained by using an international trade analogy. Labor has observable characteristics X which are valued at some price δ_0 in the country of origin and at price δ_1 in the country of destination. Income-maximizing persons will "sell" the characteristic X in the labor market that attaches a higher price to that characteristic. Hence X-intensive labor is exported to the country that has a high price for X.

An analysis complementary to the economic model of selection summarized by equations (4) and (5) can be derived if it is assumed that the vector X consists of only one variable, say education (denoted by s), and that this variable, too, is normally distributed in the population. The assumption of only one variable in the vector X is not important, since the results can be generalized to any number of variables; it is used here simply for pedagogical reasons. The assumption of normality, though unrealistic for some socioeconomic characteristics, does simplify the mathematics substantially and allows a useful generalization of the selectivity approach to the determination of the income distribution of immigrants.

The earnings functions in the two countries are now given by:

$$\ln \omega_0 - \mu_0 + \delta_0 s + \epsilon_0, \tag{9}$$

$$\ln \omega_1 - \mu_1 + \delta_1 s + \epsilon_1. \tag{10}$$

The coefficients of schooling δ_0 and δ_1 can be interpreted as "rates of return" to schooling, and give the rate at which the earnings of individuals increase as more schooling is obtained.

Suppose the distribution of educational attainment in the population of the country of origin can be written as:

$$s = \mu_s + \epsilon_s \tag{11}$$

where ϵ_s is normally distributed with mean zero and variance σ_s^2. Note that the mean education level of persons in the country of origin is given by μ_s.

Since individuals migrate when the index variable I is greater than zero, it is instructive to calculate the conditional mean $E(s \mid I > 0)$. This conditional mean gives the average education level of migrants. Using the normality assumption, it can be shown that this conditional mean is given by:

$$E(s \mid I > 0) = \mu_s + (\delta_1 - \delta_0)\lambda' \tag{12}$$

where λ' is a positive number. Note that the conditional mean in (12) is composed of two terms. The first is the mean of schooling in the population of the country of origin (μ_s), while the second is the "selectivity bias" indicating the extent to which the schooling of migrants differs from the average schooling level in the country of origin. Equation (12) reveals that the mean schooling level of migrants will be less than or greater than the mean schooling level of the population in the country of origin depending on which of the two countries values schooling more. Positive selection in schooling occurs when the migrant flow is mainly composed of highly educated individuals. Equation (12) shows this will occur when $(\delta_1 - \delta_0) > 0$, so that the labor market in the host country attaches a higher value to schooling. Conversely, negative selection in schooling occurs when the migrant flow is mainly composed of persons with low education levels. This will occur when $(\delta_1 - \delta_0) < 0$, so that highly educated individuals have little incentive to leave a country which has a higher ''rate of return'' to schooling than the country of destination.

It is remarkable that these selection conditions have *nothing* whatsoever to do with the selection conditions determining the level of abilities or unobserved characteristics in the migrant population. Recall that selection on the basis of unobserved characteristics depends entirely on the extent of income inequality in the countries of origin and destination, and in the correlation coefficient in earnings across the two countries. Any permutation of selection mechanisms in unobserved and observed characteristics is, therefore, theoretically possible. That is, negative selection in unobserved characteristics (or ability) may be occurring simultaneously with positive selection to education, or vice versa; the migrant flow originating in country 0 may be composed of relatively highly-educated persons, but these highly educated persons do not do well in the country of destination and did not do well in the country of origin (relative to other highly educated persons) prior to their migration. An important insight, therefore, is that an empirical observation that the migrant flow to any given host country is composed of mainly highly-educated individuals *does not* imply that these highly-educated persons are the most productive highly-educated persons in the country of origin.

This important implication of the economic theory of immigration reveals that little can be learned from comparisons of average earnings between migrants and natives in any host country. These comparisons incorporate the differences in both observed and unobserved characteristics that affect earnings, and confound two types of selections that characterize the migrant flow. Simply because the average migrant earns more than the average native does not imply a positive selection of the migrant population. This observation is consistent with a positive selection in observed characteristics (such as education), and a negative selection in abilities or unobserved variables. Similarly, the observation that migrants perform worse than natives does not by itself imply that the migrant population is negatively selected. This empirical observation is consistent with negative selection in the observed characteristics (the migrants may have little education), but strong positive selection in the unobserved characteristics (they are the most able persons in the population of low-educated workers). The analysis, therefore, provides an important theoretical reason for focusing on the study of *standardized* comparisons between immigrants and natives. These standardized comparisons, which hold constant differences in education, age, etc. across the groups, provide measures of the types of selections in unobserved characteristics and can, therefore, be interpreted within the framework of the economic theory of immigration. The remainder of this monograph focuses on these types of comparisons, and the next chapter will present a framework that allows the measurement of these differences in unobserved characteristics.

NOTES

[1]The model will be presented in a heuristic fashion. A formal presentation of the model, including proofs and discussions of technical details, is given in Borjas (1987a, 1987b).

[2]It is possible that the valuation the country of destination attaches to the socioeconomic characteristics of the immigrant population differs from the valuation attached to the characteristics of country 1 natives. The differences in these "rates of return" between natives and immigrants may arise due to discrimination against the race or ethnic characteristics of foreign-born persons or to other unobserved factors (e.g., the quality of schooling is different in the country of origin and in the country of destination). To keep the presentation of the model simple, these issues are ignored in what follows but they are relatively easy to incorporate into the model without affecting any of the substantive results. See Borjas (1987b).

[3]The derivation of equations (4) and (5) crucially depends on the assumption that the ratio of mobility costs to earnings (C/ω_0) is constant across individuals. Clearly, the level of migration costs C is likely to vary across individuals. For example, there are time costs associated with migration, and these time costs are likely to be higher for persons with higher opportunity costs. In addition, there are transportation costs associated with migration, and these direct costs include not only the air fare (which is likely to be relatively constant across individuals), but also moving and resettlement expenses of family and household goods, and it may be reasonable to suppose that these expenses may also be a positive function of ω_0. These hypotheses give little hint as to how the ratio of mobility costs to earnings varies across individuals. It is instructive to assume that this ratio is constant across individuals since the main implications of the theory are clearest in this special case. It can be shown (Borjas 1987b) that the treatment of this ratio as a random variable in the population does not

substantially alter the analysis, and will, under some conditions, reinforce the conclusions of the simpler model.

[4]The constant $\bar{\kappa}$ is defined as

$$\min \left(\frac{\sigma_1}{\sigma_0}, \frac{\sigma_0}{\sigma_1} \right).$$

4

Empirical Framework

As noted in chapter 1, recent empirical work analyzing the determinants of immigrant earnings has stressed the importance of differentiating between cohort, aging (or assimilation), and period effects.[1] Suppose two census cross-sections (e.g., the 1970 and 1980 U.S. Censuses) are available in a particular host country, and the following regression model is estimated:

$$\ln \omega_{ij} = X_j \delta_i + \alpha_1 y_j + \alpha_2 y_j^2 + \sum_t \beta_t C_t + \gamma_i \pi_j + \epsilon_{ij}, \quad (13)$$

$$\ln \omega_{n\ell} = X_\ell \delta_n + \gamma_n \pi_\ell + \epsilon_{n\ell} \quad (14)$$

where ω_{ij} is the earnings of immigrant j, $\omega_{n\ell}$ is the earnings of native person ℓ; X is a vector of socioeconomic characteristics (e.g., education, age, etc.); y is a variable measuring the number of years that the immigrant has resided in the host country; C is a vector of dummy variables indicating the calendar year in which the migration occurred; and π is a dummy variable set to unity if the observation is drawn from the 1980 Census, and zero otherwise. The vector of parameters (α_1, α_2), along with the age coefficients in the vector X, provides a measure of the assimilation effect (i.e., the rate at which the age/earnings profile of immigrants is converging to the age/earnings profiles of natives), while the vector of parameters β estimates the cohort effects. The period effects are given by γ_i for immigrants and by γ_n for natives.

The structural parameters in equations (13) and (14) identify three different factors which determine immigrant earnings over time: aging, cohort, and period effects. Earnings change as a result of the aging process and this growth is captured by the coefficients of the age variable (in the vector X), and by the years-since-migration variable y. These coefficients can be used to trace out the age/earnings profile of immigrants in the host country. In addition, the age coefficients in the native earnings function can also be used to trace out the age/earnings profiles of natives in the host country. The comparison of the two age/earnings profiles will lead to an estimate of immigration "assimilation" or adaptation (i.e., the rate at which the two age/earnings profiles converge).

Equation (13) also includes a vector of variables indicating the calendar year in which migration occurred, *holding constant the length of residence in the host country*. The coefficient vector β gives the cohort effects and measures the rate of change in earnings capacities across successive immigrant waves. This coefficient vector, therefore, will provide important insights into the secular changes in the selection mechanism that sorts immigrants across the host countries. Finally, equations (13) and (14) allow for the possibility that changes in aggregate economic conditions, or period effects, have a differential impact on immigrant and native earnings (i.e., γ_i may differ from γ_n). The differences in period effects can arise because, for instance, immigrant earnings may be more sensitive to changes in economic conditions.

It is well known that the three effects contained in equations (13) and (14) are not identified unless some normalization is made about either the aging, cohort, or period effects (Heckman and Robb 1983). In other words, two cross-sections cannot identify three separate sets of coefficients, and something must be assumed about one of the effects in order to identify the other two. One reasonable normalization is that the period effect experienced by immigrants (γ_i) is identical to the period effect experienced by natives (γ_n). In other words, changes in earnings due to shifts in aggregate economic conditions affect the immigrant and native wage levels by the same relative magnitude. This normalization, of course, implies that the wage *differential* between immigrants and natives is invariant to the business cycle.

The model in equations (13) and (14) will be estimated using both U.S. and Canadian data since two censuses are available for each of the two host countries. Unfortunately, only one cross-section is available for Australia, and a somewhat different methodology (discussed below) will be used for that host country. The estimates of these earnings structures can be used to infer the kinds of selections in unobserved ability that characterize the migration flows into the various host countries. There are two dimensions of migrant "quality" that can be calculated from the estimated regressions: (a) the entry wage of immigrants when they arrive into the host country; and (b) the rate at which this wage changes as the immigrants age. In addition, it is easy to combine these two measures of quality into a single number measuring the relative life-cycle wealth of immigrants. In particular, let $\bar{\omega}_i(\theta)$ be the entry wage of an immigrant who arrives in the host country at age 20 in calendar year θ, and let $\bar{\omega}_n$ be the entry wage of a similarly skilled native person (in terms of all the observable socioeconomic characteristics) who enters the labor market at age 20. Similarly, let g_i be the rate at which the earnings of immigrants grow over the life cycle, and let g_n be the growth rate for natives. Finally, let r be the rate of discount (assumed to be the same for migrants and natives). If persons are infinitely lived, the present values associated with the earnings profiles of migrants and natives are given by:

$$V_i(\theta) = \int_0^\infty \bar{\omega}_i(\theta)e^{-(r-g_i)t} \, dt = \bar{\omega}_i(\theta)/(r-g_i), \qquad (15)$$

$$V_n = \int_0^\infty \bar{\omega}_n e^{-(r-g_n)t} \, dt = \bar{\omega}_n(r-g_n). \qquad (16)$$

Equations (15) and (16) provide a summary measure of the life-cycle wealth of each immigrant cohort and of comparable natives. In other words, it "adds up" earnings at each point of the working life cycle for immigrants and natives after discounting future earnings at rate r. These summary statistics, therefore, provide valuable information about the economic welfare of immigrant cohorts relative to comparable natives.

It can be shown that an approximation to the percentage differential in the present value of earnings between migrants of cohort θ and natives is given by:

$$\ln (V_i(\theta)/V_n) = (\ln \bar{\omega}_i(\theta) - \ln \bar{\omega}_n) + \frac{g_i - g_n}{r} \qquad (17)$$

This present value differential can be easily evaluated by using the regression coefficients estimated in equations (13) and (14) if two additional assumptions are made. First, the rate of discount is assumed to be 5 percent. Clearly, the assumption of any higher rate of discount would reduce the importance of earnings later in the life cycle (where immigrants tend to do relatively better if any assimilation takes place), and hence would lead to a *decline* in relative immigrant earnings. Second, the growth rates g_i and g_n must be evaluated from the age and years-since-migration coefficients in the earnings functions. The quadratic specification of age and years-since-migration in the earnings functions implies that the growth rate is not constant over time. The empirical analysis below will define the growth rates g_i and g_n by:

$$\hat{g}_i = [Y_i(\bar{X}, 50, 30, \theta) - Y_i(\bar{X}, 20, 0, \theta)]/30, \qquad (18)$$

$$\hat{g}_n = [Y_n(\bar{X}, 50) - Y_n(\bar{X}, 20)]/30, \qquad (19)$$

where $Y_i(X, A, y, \theta)$ is the predicted (ln) earnings for an immigrant with characteristics X, at age A, with y years of residence, and who migrated to the host country in calendar year θ. Similarly, $Y_n(X, A)$ gives the predicted earnings for a native with characteristics X at age A. Equations (18) and (19), therefore, define the growth rates as the average percentage increase in earnings experienced by immigrants and comparable natives between ages 20 and 50 (evaluated at the mean characteristic of the migrant population, $\bar{X}$).

This approach has the important property that the growth rates are a linear function of regression coefficients, and since the entry wages are given by $Y_i(\bar{X}, 20, 0, \theta)$ for immigrants and $Y_n(\bar{X}, 20)$ for natives, the present value differential in (17) is also a linear function of regression coefficients, and standard errors can be easily evaluated. Hence the methodological framework presented in this chapter provides a simple way of calculating summary measures of immigrant labor market performance and of evaluating the statistical significance of these summary measures.

It is important to stress that this approach marks a significant departure from the empirical tradition in the literature which analyzes immigrant earnings. This entire literature is essentially concerned with the estimation of entry wage levels and with the calculation of "overtaking" points (if they exist). This type of analysis is misleading or irrelevant if overtaking points occur rather late in the life cycle or if they do not occur at all, as some recent evidence suggests. The empirical use of the present value of earnings is much more consistent with the theory of migration presented in the last chapter and de-emphasizes the somewhat misleading concept of overtaking points. Analysis of the success of migrant groups in any host country, to borrow from human capital theory, which guided much early research on immigrant earnings, should not be based on the comparison of wage differentials at given ages, but on comparisons of the life cycle wealth accumulated by similar migrants and natives. Hence the present value approach used in the empirical sections of this monograph is much more in the tradition of the human capital literature and of the economic theory of immigration.

NOTES

[1]The importance of distinguishing between cohort and aging effects was first stressed in the immigration literature by Borjas (1985). In that paper, I show how cross-section regressions of immigrant earnings on the variable years-since-migration do not provide any useful information about the extent of assimilation of immigrants in the host country's labor market.

5

Data

The data used in the empirical analysis presented in this monograph are drawn from Public Use Samples of the censuses conducted in each of the destination countries: the United States, Canada, and Australia. The last two U.S. censuses (and the only recent ones that contain information on when persons migrated to the United States) were conducted in 1970 and 1980. The immigrant extract drawn from the 1970 Census is a $\frac{2}{100}$ random sample of the 1970 foreign-born population (obtained by pooling the $\frac{1}{100}$ 5 percent SMSA and County Group File with the $\frac{1}{100}$ 5 percent State File). The 1980 data for immigrants residing in the U.S. is a $\frac{5}{100}$ random sample of the foreign-born population (available in the A File of the 1980 Public Use Sample). *All* immigrant observations that satisfy the restrictions of being prime-age men (aged 25–64), who are not self-employed, whose records report at least $1000 in annual earnings in the year prior to the Census, and who are not residing in group quarters are used in the analysis below. These sample restrictions, of course, lead to very large sample sizes for immigrants and even larger sample sizes for native persons (if the same sampling proportions are used). Hence random samples of the Public Use files are drawn for the U.S. native extracts used in the analysis.[1]

The Canadian censuses were conducted in 1971 and 1981. Both of these Censuses (like the U.S.) have the important characteristic that they report the year in which foreign-born persons migrated to Canada. The 1971 data for both immigrants and natives residing in Canada is a $\frac{1}{100}$ random sample of the Canadian population, while the 1981 file is a $\frac{2}{100}$ random sample of the Canadian population. Again, all observations (for both immigrants and natives) that satisfy the restrictions of being prime-age men, not self-employed, not in group quarters, and whose records report positive annual earnings in the year prior to the census are included in the empirical analysis below.

Finally, the Australian data used in this paper are drawn from the 1981 Australian Census of Population and Housing. This census file is a $\frac{1}{100}$ random sample of the Australian population, and the entire sample for both immigrants and natives that satisfies the restriction on sex, age, self-employment, etc., is used below.

Three important problems are raised by the Australian data. First, only one census is available and, therefore, the aging/cohort decomposition presented in chapter 4 cannot be conducted. Thus Australian results are not directly comparable to those obtained for the other two countries. Nevertheless, a simple and intuitive solution which allows some rough comparisons will be proposed below. Second, the Australian census does not report annual earnings, but instead reports annual incomes (which include nonsalary receipts). The problem may not be very serious since self-employed persons are omitted from the study, and these are the individuals who are most likely to have large receipts of nonwage income. Finally, the Australian census (unlike the U.S. and Canadian data sets) does not contain good measures of labor supply. Hence a wage rate for the year prior to the census cannot be calculated. The empirical analysis in this monograph, therefore, will be conducted on the logarithm of annual earnings. It is important to note, however, that the analysis for both the U.S. and Canada was replicated using the wage rate as the dependent variable, with little change in the qualitative nature of the results.

Table 5.1 presents summary statistics (mean log earnings and education) as well as sample sizes for the various samples that will be used in the analysis. In addition, table 5.1 decomposes the immigrant population in each of the host countries in terms of the continent of origin. This decomposition by continent (rather than by country) is mandated by the fact that for Australia and Canada, the decomposition by country leads to a very small number of observations for most countries. In addition, the Canadian censuses identify the country of origin only for a select group of (Western) European immigrants. Hence the decomposition presented in table 5.1 is the only comparable

Table 5.1 Summary Statistics in Immigrant and Native Samples

Country of destination

United States

Country of origin	1970			1980		
	ℓn(w)	EDUC	N	ℓn(w)	EDUC	N
Natives	8.99	11.5	28978	9.61	12.7	15071
Asia	8.88	13.3	3495	9.47	14.6	25288
Africa	8.88	13.9	172	9.40	15.3	2622
Europe	9.06	10.8	16922	9.69	12.1	42734
Latin America	8.67	9.2	7507	9.23	9.4	48929
All Immigrants	8.95	10.8	32491	9.46	11.7	134252

Canada

Country of origin	1971			1981		
	ℓn(w)	EDUC	N	ℓn(w)	EDUC	N
Natives	8.82	9.9	28049	9.79	11.3	61205
Asia	8.72	13.2	409	9.66	13.6	2372
Africa	8.86	14.1	119	9.74	14.0	504
Europe	8.86	10.0	6633	9.86	10.9	12193
Latin America	8.72	12.0	223	9.60	12.1	1229
All Immigrants	8.86	10.5	8018	9.81	11.7	17417

Australia

Country of origin	1981		
	ℓn(w)	EDUC	N
Natives	9.39	11.6	23086
Asia	9.34	12.9	1074
Africa	9.45	13.1	267
Europe	9.34	11.4	7799
Latin America	9.35	12.1	102
All Immigrants	9.36	11.7	9936

decomposition available for non-European immigrants across the countries of destination.

The results presented in table 5.1 for the United States show a downward trend in the earnings of immigrants (relative to natives) over the decade. The average immigrant in 1970 earned, on average, about as much as the typical native worker. By 1980, however, immigrant earnings were about 15 percent below the native wage. Undoubtedly, part of this decline in the relative immigrant wage is due to the fact that a larger share of immigrants in 1980 originate in Asian, African, and Latin American countries. It is well known that non-European immigrants tend not to perform well in the U.S. labor market. However, table 5.1 documents that the relative decline in the immigrant wage is also exhibited by immigrants from a given continent. For example, the average wage of African immigrants in 1970 was 11 percent below that of natives, while by 1980 the gap had widened to a 21 percent difference.

The Canadian results, at this aggregate level, show little change in the relative earnings of immigrants between 1971 and 1981. In both censuses, the average immigrant had slightly higher earnings than the typical native worker. Within continents, however, a marked change in relative immigrant earnings is documented for persons originating in Latin America: their earnings were about 10 percent below those of Canadian natives in 1971, but by 1981 the differential was 19 percent.

Finally, the Australian statistics show that the typical immigrant in 1981 had about the same level of earnings as the typical native. Unlike the U.S. and Canada, however, the relative earnings of immigrants vary little by country of origin, with the exception being the relatively small sample of immigrants originating in Africa. Surprisingly, these migrants perform much better than all other immigrant groups and natives.

It is very instructive to compare the 1981 relative earnings of Australian immigrants with the relevant numbers for Canada and the United States. Consider, for instance, the sample of immigrants that originated in Europe. Those residing in Australia actually have the *lowest* average earnings of any of the Australian immigrant groups, and have a wage disadvantage of about 5 percent despite the fact that their education level is roughly the same as that of natives. In Canada, on the other hand, European immigrants tend to have higher earnings than any of the other groups, even though their education level, if anything, is slightly lower than that of natives. Finally, in the U.S.,

European immigrants outperform all other immigrant groups, even though they have about half a year of schooling less than natives. This comparison thus reveals the role of the immigration market in nonrandomly allocating the population of European migrants across the three countries of destination.

This result is also indicated by the comparison of the various groups of Asian immigrants across the host countries in 1980–1981. It was shown earlier that the Asian immigrant cohorts had increased significantly in size in all three host countries. Asians who migrated to the U.S. tend to be highly-educated (about two more years of schooling than natives), and do not perform well in the labor market. Their earnings disadvantage is roughly 14 percent. Asians in Canada also have more education than natives (about 2.3 years more), and their earnings disadvantage is roughly 13 percent. On the other hand, Asians in Australia have about 1.3 years more schooling than natives, but their earnings disadvantage relative to natives is only 5 percent. Hence the selection biases generated by the nonrandom sorting of migrants with host countries leads to Asian immigrants being positively selected in terms of schooling, but some host countries seem to be getting more productive Asians, in terms of unobserved skills, than other host countries.

An important insight is suggested by the aggregate statistics presented in table 5.1: generalizations about the productivity or earnings capacities of ethnic or national origin groups are likely to be misleading since they ignore the self-selectivity that generated the composition of the migrant pool in each of the host countries. In other words, there is no such thing as "the" impact of Asian ethnicity or race on immigrant earnings. The value attached by the host country's labor market to ethnic or racial characteristics depends greatly on the kinds of selections that generated the particular flow of immigrants. In some host countries, Asian "ethnicity" will imply relatively high earnings and successful labor market outcomes, while in other countries the same label will be associated with relatively low earnings and unsuccessful labor market outcomes. There is no general "law" suggesting that a racial/ethnic label must be associated with higher or lower earnings. The key determinant of the labor market success of any immigrant group will be the kinds of selection that generated the migration flow in the first place, and the type of sorting that dispersed the emigrants across the various host countries.

NOTES

[1]The 1970 native extract is a .001 sample from the population, while the 1980 native extract is a .0042 sample from the population.

6

1980–1981
Cross-Section Results

It is instructive to begin the analysis by presenting the earnings functions estimated in the 1980/1981 cross-sections in each of the destination countries. These regressions—estimated separately in the samples of natives and immigrants—are presented in table 6.1. The regressions in the native sample are of interest mainly because they are so similar across the three destination countries. The coefficients of age, marital status, and urbanization status all have the expected signs and are of similar magnitudes whether the labor market is in Australia, Canada, or the United States. For instance, the age coefficient is .084 in the United States, .087 in Canada, and .089 in Australia. These differences are not only statistically insignificant, but numerically trivial. The only coefficient in the native earnings functions that seems to be an outlier is the coefficient of education in Australia. The coefficient of education in the United States and in Canada is between .05 and .06, indicating that an additional year of education increases earnings by about 5 to 6 percent in each of these two labor markets. The Australian earnings function, on the other hand, has a coefficient for education that exceeds .09. This result indicates that the Australian labor market values higher levels of education much more than the labor markets in either of the other two host countries.

The cross-section regressions on immigrant earnings presented in table 6.1 are estimated in the samples containing all foreign-born persons in each of the countries of destination. The regressions were also estimated in the various immigrant subsamples by region of origin. These regressions are not presented to conserve space, but summary statistics derived from these equations will be presented and discussed below. The comparisons of the earnings functions in the

Table 6.1   1980/1981 Cross-Section Regressions in Host Countries (Dependent Variable = ln Annual Earnings)

| | Country of destination | | | | | |
| | USA | | Canada | | Australia | |
Sample:	Coeff.	t	Coeff.	t	Coeff.	t
Natives:						
CONSTANT	6.6488	(76.33)	7.0465	(193.01)	6.3522	(104.68)
EDUC	.0587	(33.92)	.0510	(76.26)	.0908	(58.77)
AGE	.0841	(20.17)	.0873	(49.42)	.0886	(32.01)
AGE^2	−.0009	(−18.00)	−.0009	(−45.21)	−.0011	(−34.61)
MAR	.3151	(23.53)	.2973	(51.10)	.2727	(31.31)
HLTH	−.3337	(−15.15)	—	—	—	—
URBAN	.1545	(12.07)	.1036	(22.78)	.1605	(16.61)
R^2	.193		.171		.245	
All Immigrants:						
CONSTANT	6.6378	(223.77)	7.3415	(95.72)	6.7307	(66.17)
EDUC	.0497	(133.61)	.0415	(40.97)	.0748	(35.59)
AGE	.0802	(55.39)	.0710	(19.31)	.0779	(16.86)
AGE^2	−.0009	(−51.35)	−.0008	(−18.44)	−.0010	(−18.70)
MAR	.2325	(50.52)	.2190	(18.42)	.2013	(14.16)
HLTH	−.3502	(−34.48)	—	—	—	—
URBAN	.0574	(9.43)	−.0016	(−.16)	.1079	(5.41)
Y70	.2107	(36.81)	.1609	(9.73)	.0444	(2.11)
Y65	.3141	(51.89)	.2816	(18.03)	.0491	(2.36)
Y60	.3750	(56.74)	.2825	(15.39)	.0810	(3.68)
Y50	.4436	(74.88)	.3679	(25.59)	.0811	(4.18)
Y40	.4752	(64.63)	.4287	(17.50)	.1159	(4.63)
R^2	.226		.163		.188	

Key to Variables: EDUC = years of completed schooling; MAR = 1 if married, spouse present; HTLH = 1 if health limits work; SMSA = 1 if resident of metropolitan area; Y70 = 1 if migrated in 1970–74; Y65 = 1 if migrated in 1965–69; Y60 = 1 if migrated in 1960–64; Y50 = 1 if migrated in 1950–59; and Y40 = 1 if migrated prior to 1950.

pooled immigrant samples across host countries also show that the impact of education on the earnings of foreign-born persons in Australia is higher than the impact of education on the earnings of foreign-born persons in either Canada or the United States.

Of more substantive interest, however, is the general result that practically all socioeconomic variables (i.e., education, age, marital status, and urbanization) have a *smaller* impact on the earnings of immigrants than on the earnings of natives *regardless of the country of destination.* For instance, the education coefficients are about 1 percentage point higher in the native samples than in the immigrant samples; the coefficients of age are about 1–2 percentage points higher; the coefficients of marital status are about 7–8 percentage points higher; and the coefficients of urbanization are about 5–10 percentage points higher. Thus the earnings of immigrants are much less responsive to socioeconomic characteristics than the earnings of natives in these market economies.

One interpretation of this substantive finding is that the host country's labor market does not impute a relatively high price to the skills and signals associated with these socioeconomic variables for immigrants. Education and age, for instance, partly measure skills obtained prior to migration, and hence the host country's labor market does not completely reward immigrants for schooling and labor market experience obtained abroad. Similarly, the urbanization of immigrants probably does not reflect the same kinds of selection biases that are implicit in the urbanization of natives.

Finally, the immigrant regressions in table 6.1 include a vector of dummy variables indicating the time of immigration. The five variables in this vector are: Y70 (= 1 if the migration occurred in 1970–1974, 0 otherwise), Y65 (= 1 if the migration occurred in 1965–1969, 0 otherwise), Y60 (= 1 if the migration occurred in 1960–1964, 0 otherwise), Y50 (= 1 if the migration occurred in 1950–1959, 0 otherwise), and Y40 (= 1 if the migration occurred prior to 1950, 0 otherwise). The omitted dummy variable indexes whether the migration occurred in the post-1975 period.[1] The variables in this vector tend to have a predictable effect: they are positive and tend to be larger the earlier the migration occurred. In other words, the earnings of immigrants who have resided in the host country for many years are higher than the earnings of more recent immigrants. It is of importance to note, however, that these coefficients tend to have roughly equal magnitudes in Canada and the United States, but that the cross-section regression in the Australian census indicates a rather small effect of length of residence on the earnings of foreign-born persons in Australia. This discrepancy across the host countries has major substantive implications and will be discussed in detail below.

Of course, an important use of these cross-section regressions is to predict the size of the wage differentials between immigrants and natives for each of the cohorts. These predictions are calculated using the mean socioeconomic characteristics of the immigrant sample in each of the host countries. In addition, these predictions are obtained by holding the age of immigration constant at age 20 *for all cohorts.* Hence the typical immigrant in the 1975–1980 cohort would be 23 years old, the typical immigrant in the 1970–1974 cohort would be 28 years old, etc. It should be clear from the discussion in chapter 4 that this methodology ensures that the wage differentials thus obtained from cross-section regressions incorporate both cohort and aging effects. For example, the wage differential calculated for the 1970–1974 cohort incorporates the fact that this cohort arrived in that period, as well as the fact that it has aged in the country of residence, so that the wage differential is evaluated at mean age 28. The predictions obtained from the immigrant sample can be compared to the predicted earnings that natives obtain at the relevant ages, and thus a *relative* immigrant wage can be calculated for each of the cohorts. The predicted relative wages are presented in the top panel of table 6.2 for the pooled sample of immigrants in each of the host countries.

Table 6.2 shows that the U.S. and Canadian cross-section relative earnings profiles resemble the ones usually reported in the literature. Earnings for the most recent cohorts, relative to the earnings of similar (in terms of education, age, etc.) natives, are relatively low. In the 1980 U.S. census, for example, the most recent immigrants have 34.6 percent lower earnings than natives, while the respective statistic for Canada is 22.7 percent. The earlier cohorts, either because they are older and have been in the country a longer time (and thus had more time to assimilate), or because there are vintage or cohort effects, do much better in the labor market. For example, cohorts arriving in 1950–1959 in either the U.S. or Canada have essentially reached earnings parity with, if not surpassed, native earnings.

The top panel of table 6.2, however, clearly shows that the Australian experience in the pooled sample of immigrants is very different. The 1981 Australian cross-section does not indicate any evidence that the earnings of immigrants (relative to similar natives)

Table 6.2   Earnings Differentials Between Immigrants and Natives in 1980–81 Cross-Sections

Origin and destination	Immigrant cohort					
	1975–80	1970–74	1965–69	1960–64	1950–59	<1950
All immigrants in:						
USA	−.3460	−.1534	−.0676	−.0239	.0177	.0045
	(−14.48)	(−10.42)	(−6.91)	(−2.58)	(1.79)	(.39)
Canada	−.2271	−.1118	−.0286	−.0571	−.0020	.0558
	(−9.52)	(−6.61)	(−2.35)	(−3.99)	(−.22)	(2.78)
Australia	−.0810	−.0642	−.0814	−.0656	−.0796	−.0342
	(−2.51)	(−2.87)	(−4.98)	(−4.05)	(−6.06)	(−1.82)
African immigrants in:						
USA	−.6275	−.1778	−.0556	−.0571	−.0271	.0070
	(−8.21)	(−2.58)	(−.74)	(−1.26)	(−.81)	(.22)
Canada	−.7785	−.4723	−.2320	.0536	.0899	−.0875
	(−2.89)	(−1.54)	(−1.37)	(.28)	(1.81)	(−1.10)
Australia	−.0631	−.2862	−.5510	−.3518	−.0976	−.0317
	(−.17)	(−.62)	(−2.35)	(−1.09)	(−1.00)	(−.52)
Asian immigrants in:						
USA	−.2554	.1702	.1992	.1058	.1150	.0873
	(−3.91)	(3.41)	(5.18)	(3.42)	(4.35)	(3.55)
Canada	.0831	−.1321	.1281	−.0921	.0200	.0036
	(.42)	(−.73)	(1.08)	(−1.03)	(.41)	(.01)
Australia	−.7010	−.1620	−.2946	.1679	.0799	.0753
	(−2.60)	(−.60)	(−1.16)	(.96)	(.89)	(1.07)
European immigrants in:						
USA	−.2287	−.0638	.0366	.0781	.1042	.0814
	(−8.52)	(−3.57)	(2.99)	(6.78)	(10.13)	(6.76)
Canada	−.0406	.0195	.0009	−.0472	.0101	.0574
	(−1.32)	(.83)	(.01)	(−2.97)	(1.05)	(2.49)
Australia	.0002	−.0207	−.0709	−.0685	−.0750	−.0416
	(.14)	(−.79)	(−3.88)	(−3.99)	(−5.45)	(−2.09)
Latin American immigrants in:						
USA	−.3509	−.1815	−.0713	.0842	.1254	.0348
	(−2.18)	(−1.66)	(−1.10)	(1.02)	(2.60)	(.87)
Canada	−.0417	−.2951	−.1652	−.0727	−.0611	−.0318
	(−.10)	(−1.02)	(−1.44)	(−.24)	(−.61)	(−.32)
Australia	.2330	.6214	−.0310	−.0652	−.2076	−.2244
	(.61)	(1.46)	(−.17)	(−.24)	(−1.24)	(−1.35)

NOTE: The t-ratios are presented in parentheses.

increase substantially with age. The relative earnings of immigrants in Australia hover around 7–8 percent less than the earnings of natives, and there is no discernible trend as individuals age. This remarkable empirical finding implies an important substantive result: if there is *any* assimilation effect in Australia (i.e., if the earnings of immigrants rise at a faster rate than the earnings of natives) the 1981 Australian cross-section must imply that the quality of immigrants to Australia *increased* in the 1960–1980 period. This insight can be easily seen by asking the following question: How can it be that the most recent immigrants in Australia earn about as much as immigrants who arrived in Australia decades earlier and are much older? If there is any assimilation effect, this puzzle can be resolved only if the quality or labor market productivity of recent immigrants to Australia greatly exceeds the labor market productivity of earlier waves of immigrants.

It is important to note that even in the extreme case in which foreign-born persons in Australia experience no assimilation whatsoever, the Australian experience would still differ markedly from that of the United States. Borjas (1985) has documented a sizable decline in the quality of immigrants admitted to the U.S. over the same period. If there are no assimilation effects, the cross-section profile provides a correct measure of cohort effects, and the Australian results in the top panel of table 6.2 show that there has been little change in average earnings of immigrant cohorts over time. Hence at the same time that the quality of persons migrating to the U.S. has been declining, the quality of persons choosing Australia as their destination either remained constant or increased. Thus a simple comparison of the cross-section regressions across the destination countries leads to an important insight into the trends that mark the nonrandom sorting of immigrants across the three host countries over the last 20–30 years.

The remaining panels of table 6.2 calculate the relative earnings for each of the immigrant cohorts in the cross-section by continent of origin. The immigrant earnings functions presented in table 6.1 were reestimated separately for each of the continents of origin, and these regressions (along with the means for the immigrant samples for each of the continents) were then used to predict the relative earnings of immigrant cohorts in the various national origin groups. The results in table 6.2 show that, in general, the earnings of immigrants residing in the U.S. exhibit similar cross-sectional patterns regardless of the continent of origin. Consider, for instance, the group of European immigrants. The 1980 U.S. census cross-section reveals that the most recent European immigrants earn 22.9 percent less than comparable natives, while immigrants who arrived in the U.S. in the 1960–64 period earn about 7.8 percent *more* than natives. Similarly, the study of Latin American immigrants shows that the most recent Latin American immigrants do quite badly in the U.S. labor market (earning 35.1 percent less than comparable natives), but that the older immigrants who arrived prior to 1950 do relatively well in the labor market (earning 12.5 percent more than natives).

As with the pooled sample, the results obtained from the Australian census also tend to indicate that the quality of foreign-born persons choosing Australia as their destination has either remained constant or increased over the last two decades. For instance, the 1981 Australian cross-section shows that the most recently arrived European immigrants have essentially the same earnings as comparable natives, but that earlier waves of European immigrants earn less than natives. The 1965–1969 cohort of European immigrants in Australia, for instance, earns about 7.1 percent less than natives. To the extent that any assimilation takes place, these cross-section results indicate that cohort effects among European immigrants in Australia are quite sizable.

Unlike the results obtained in the pooled sample, the intra-continent analysis in the 1981 Canadian census does *not* yield the result that the most recent waves of immigrants systematically earn less than the earlier waves. Consider, again, the sample of European immigrants. Practically all the European immigrants who arrived in Canada since 1965 earn about the same as natives. The cross-section regression thus reveals that very little growth has taken place, or that cohort effects (with the more recent waves being more productive than the earlier waves) are dominating the analysis. The results for Asian immigrants also tend to exhibit little difference (in terms of statistical significance) across the various cohorts. These findings suggest that the pooled results reported in the top panel of table 6.2 for the Canadian census are perhaps due to the fact that the national origin composition of the

Canadian foreign-born population has changed drastically over time, away from European immigrants and towards Asian or Latin American immigrants. To the extent that Asian or Latin American immigrants do not perform as well in the labor market as European immigrants, earnings comparisons across cohorts in the pooled sample of foreign-born persons residing in Canada may be capturing this compositional change. This insight will be studied in more detail below.

NOTES

[1]There are some slight variations in the calendar years bracketed by these dummy variables across the three countries of destination. The various censuses report the year of migration in different ways, and thus the brackets reported in the text are those that apply to U.S. data. The Canadian and Australian brackets are quite similar for post-1960 migrants but differ somewhat for pre-1960 migrants.

7

Cohort and Assimilation Effects

As noted in chapter 4, two censuses are required to identify aging and cohort effects. The estimation of the model presented in equations (13) and (14) is, therefore, initially restricted to the U.S. and Canadian censuses. Within each host country, the earnings functions in (13) and (14) are estimated by pooling the 1970 (or 1971) and 1980 (or 1981) censuses. A proposed methodology for the study of the single cross-section available in the Australian census will be presented below.

As with the cross-section analysis presented in the previous chapter, five immigrant samples will be analyzed in each country of destination: the pooled sample, and subsamples of immigrants originating in Africa, Asia, Europe, and Latin America. For each of these samples, the system of equations in (13) and (14) is estimated using ordinary least squares after restricting the period effect in the immigrant earnings function to be the same as the period effect in the native earnings function. The native base used for comparisons with the foreign-born population is the group of men aged 25–64 born in the host country. Finally, the vector of socioeconomic characteristics included in the regressions is identical to the vector of socioeconomic characteristics included in the cross-section regressions presented in table 6.1.

The presentation of all the coefficients and standard errors calculated from these regressions is cumbersome and uninstructive. Therefore, the discussion in this chapter focuses on summary statistics calculated from the regression results. These summary statistics, defined in chapter 4, provide measures of the extent of wage differentials between a single immigrant cohort and natives both at the time of entry and over the life cycle. In addition, the estimated regressions can also be used

Table 7.1 Cohort Effects: Earnings of Immigrant Cohorts Relative to the 1975–1980 Cohort

	U.S.A.		Canada	
Origin/Cohort	Coefficient	t	Coefficient	t
All Immigrants:				
1970–74	.1428	(19.86)	.0991	(5.79)
1965–69	.1829	(20.03)	.1848	(11.78)
1960–64	.2204	(18.00)	.1665	(8.35)
1950–59	.2396	(15.35)	.1953	(8.89)
<1950	.2205	(10.45)	.2509	(8.04)
Africa:				
1970–74	.0682	(1.59)	−.0463	(−.64)
1965–69	.2354	(3.98)	.1401	(1.90)
1960–64	.2202	(2.75)	.0795	(.83)
1950–59	.1782	(1.71)	.1497	(1.14)
<1950	.1973	(1.23)	.6199	(1.39)
Asia:				
1970–74	.1267	(9.34)	.0271	(.81)
1965–69	.1126	(6.67)	.1396	(4.03)
1960–64	.1196	(4.98)	.0279	(.50)
1950–59	.0140	(.46)	.0062	(.09)
<1950	.0205	(.46)	.4566	(2.84)
Europe:				
1970–74	.0901	(6.74)	.0629	(2.36)
1965–69	.1286	(9.48)	.0537	(2.37)
1960–64	.1504	(8.90)	.0223	(.85)
1950–59	.1376	(6.79)	.0631	(2.23)
<1950	.1286	(4.93)	.0939	(2.60)
Latin America:				
1970–74	.1443	(13.94)	.0491	(1.06)
1965–69	.1473	(11.25)	.1619	(3.47)
1960–64	.1875	(11.02)	.2082	(2.94)
1950–59	.1433	(6.58)	.1555	(1.61)
<1950	.1087	(3.32)	.5100	(1.96)

to obtain measures of the wage differentials across the different immigrant cohorts (i.e., the cohort effects), and of the rate at which the earnings of immigrants are converging on the earnings of natives (i.e., the assimilation effect).

It is most useful to begin the presentation of the results by analyzing the estimated cohort effects, which are presented in table 7.1. These cohort effects measure the extent of wage differentials *as of the time of entry* into the host country's labor market across the various waves of immigrants. The statistics presented in table 7.1 are interpreted as the percentage earnings advantage (or disadvantage) of earlier immigrant waves relative to the most recent cohort (i.e., arrivals after 1975).

It is instructive to consider a specific set of results in order to understand the substantive implications of these statistics. Consider, for concreteness, the pooled sample of immigrants who migrated to the United States. Table 7.1 clearly documents that the earlier cohorts of immigrants who chose the United States as their destination have a substantial earnings advantage over the most recent cohort of immigrants who chose the United States as their destination. The 1970–1974 cohort, for example, has an entry wage 14.3 percent higher than the most recent immigrants (i.e., post-1975 arrivals). Similarly, the 1960–1964 cohort has over 20 percent higher earnings than the most recent cohort. These results, of course, are quite similar to those presented in my earlier work (Borjas 1985), which first documented the existence of a cohort quality decline in the United States over the postwar period.

It is of substantive interest that the quality decline documented for the pooled sample of immigrants in the United States basically began about 1965. Table 7.1 shows that practically all immigrants who arrived before 1964 have basically the same wage advantage over the most recent wave (the pre-1964 immigrants earn about 22–24 percent more than the post-1975 immigrants on the date of entry). Beginning with the 1965–69 cohort, however, table 7.1 reveals that the entry wage declined by about 4 percent compared to the earlier pre-1964 waves. In addition, table 7.1 documents that the decline accelerated rapidly during the 1970s.

The set of cohort coefficients calculated from the pooled sample of foreign-born persons choosing Canada as their destination is also substantively interesting. These cohort coefficients, like the United States cohort effects, reveal that the most recent immigrants have substantially lower earnings capacities than the earlier waves. The 1970–1974 cohort, for example, earns about 10 percent more than the most recent (i.e., post-1975) cohort, while the 1960–1964 cohort earns about 17 percent more than the most recent cohort. Hence a comparison of the two sets of coefficients (i.e., the U.S. and Canada cohort effects) could lead to the conclusion that the American and Canadian experiences in terms of declining cohort quality were very similar. This conclusion would be quite remarkable, particularly in light of the very different immigration policies pursued by the two host countries over the period. Recall that Canadian immigration policy is much more skill-based than U.S. immigration policy. Table 7.1 seems to indicate that the skill restrictions imposed by Canadian policy could not prevent a U.S.-like cohort quality decline.

This conclusion, however, would be erroneous. The reason for the problem can be seen in the "within-country" cohort effects presented in table 7.1. For example, consider the cohort effects calculated for immigrants of African origin. In the U.S. census, cohort effects for African immigrants are quite similar to those calculated in the pooled immigrant sample: earlier immigrant waves have lower earnings capacities than the more recent immigrant waves. On the other hand, however, the Canadian census does not reveal the existence of strong (and statistically significant) cohort effects among immigrants of African descent. The cohort parameters do not seem to follow any kind of systematic pattern and, in fact, only one of the five cohort coefficients reported in table 7.1 is statistically different from zero.

The results for the European immigrants reinforce the finding that discrepancies exist between the within-region cohort effects and the pooled cohort effects in the Canadian census. The Canadian census reveals that quality differences do exist among the various European cohorts, but that the estimated cohort effects are relatively small. Practically all cohorts that arrived between 1950 and 1975 have about 5-6 percent higher earnings than the most recent immigrant cohort (arrivals in 1975–1980). Thus there are basically no trends in the quality of European immigrants who migrated to Canada in the pre-1975 period. This finding, of course, differs considerably from the differentials estimated for the pooled Canadian sample, where cohort effects range around 15–20 percent, and where there seems to be a significant secular decline in cohort quality over the postwar period. In the U.S. census, on the other hand, the quality of European immigrant cohorts is seen to be higher for earlier waves, with quality differentials between 10–15 percent for immigrants arriving prior to 1970. Thus the U.S. within-country cohort effects again closely resemble the pooled cohort effects obtained from the analysis of the sample of pooled immigrants.

One possible factor that may be responsible for the differences in the Canadian census between the pooled cohort effects and the within-country cohort effects is the fact that the pooled cohort effects incorporate changes in the national-origin composition of the immigrant flow into Canada. The descriptive data reported earlier show that most migration to Canada during the early part of the postwar period originated in Europe. It is well known from other studies (and will be reconfirmed below) that European immigrants tend to perform quite well in the Canadian labor market. During the 1970s, however, the composition of the migrant flow shifted to incorporate more Asians and non-Europeans. It is also well known from previous studies that these types of immigrants do not tend to perform well in the Canadian labor market. Therefore, the pooled cohort effect reported in table 7.1 may be confounding two separate phenomena: (1) the impact of a changing ethnic/racial composition of the migrant flows; and (2) the impact of declining productivities (due to changes in the self-selection mechanism) among immigrants of the same national origin. In other words, the wage differential at the time of entry between "similar" natives and immigrants could have declined because the national origin composition of immigrants shifted over time towards countries that tend to perform relatively badly in the Canadian labor market.

It is easy to decompose the total quality change in terms of its two separate components. Consider:

$$R(t) = \sum_i P_i(t)\omega_i(t) \qquad (20)$$

where $\omega_i(t)$ is the average (relative) wage of immigrants from country i at time t $(t = 0,1)$; and $P_i(t)$ is the fraction of the immigrant population originating in country i at time t. The left-hand side of equation (20), by construction, gives the average wage differential between all immigrants and natives in a particular country of destination.

Table 7.2   Decomposition of Quality Change Between 1960–64 and 1975–80 Cohorts in U.S. and Canada

Destination	Average decline in earnings across cohorts	Average decline due to country of origin composition	Average decline due to within-country change in earnings capacities
U.S.A.	−.22	−.10	−.12
Canada	−.17	−.11	−.06

The change in immigrant earnings over the time period 0 to 1 can be decomposed as:

$$R(1)-R(0) = \sum_i P_i(0)[\omega_i(1)-\omega_i(0)] + \sum_i \omega_i(1)[P_i(1)-P_i(0)] \quad (21)$$

where the first term gives the change in "quality" attributable to changes in the earnings capacities of immigrants from the same country or region, while the second term gives the change in quality attributable to the fact that the national origin composition of the immigrant pool changed over that period. The pooled cohort effects presented in table 7.1 provided an estimate of the left-hand side of equation (21).

Table 7.2 presents the decomposition implied by equation (21) for the Canadian and U.S. changes in cohort quality between the 1960–64 cohort and the 1975-80 cohort. The total change in earnings capacities across cohorts in the early 1960s and late 1970s is quite similar for both countries. The earnings capacities of the 1970s immigrants is 22 percent less than the earnings capacities of the 1960–64 arrivals in the U.S., and about 17 percent less in Canada. The U.S. decomposition, however, reveals that less than half of this change (a 10 percent decline in the relative earnings capacity of immigrants) is attributable to changes in the national origin composition of the population, and that the remaining 12 percent is attributable to a decline in the earnings capacities of immigrants from the same region. On the other hand, the Canadian data reveal that over two-thirds of the change in earnings capacities over the two decades (an 11 percent decline in the relative earnings of immigrants) is attributable to changes in the national origin composition of the immigrant sample, and that only a small fraction of this decline can be attributed to changes in earnings capacities of immigrants from the same countries or regions.

The decomposition in table 7.2 shows that even though both the U.S. and Canada exhibited similar overall declines in the quality of immigrants since 1960, the *reasons* for this decline vary fundamentally across the two host countries. The decline in Canada is mostly due to the fact that more immigrants are coming from countries that tend to perform worse in the labor market, while the decline in the U.S. is, to a significant extent, caused by changes in the earnings capacities of immigrants from within the same country.

A second set of results that can be obtained from the regression estimates of equations (13) and (14) is the rate of assimilation of the immigrant population. Chapter 4 defines the rate of earnings growth of immigrants, g_i, and the rate of earnings growth of natives, g_n, as the average annual rate of growth exhibited by the earnings profiles in the first 30 years of the working life cycle (from age 20 to age 50). The difference between g_i and g_n provides an estimate of the rate of convergence in the two earnings profiles, and will be defined here as the rate of assimilation. Table 7.3 presents estimates of both g_i and g_n and of the rate of assimilation. Overall, it is seen that the assimilation rate is substantially smaller in Canada than in the United States. The earnings of immigrants in the U.S. rise at an average rate of .9 percent per year between ages 20 and 50, while in Canada they rise at a rate that's roughly half that, .4 percent per year. This surprising result is consistent with the evidence presented by Bloom and Gunderson (1987) in their study of the earnings experience of immigrants in Canada. It is unclear, however, why first-generation foreign-born persons in Canada do not seem to ''adapt'' as well to the labor market as first-generation foreign-born persons in the United States.

Table 7.3 also shows that the smaller rate of assimilation among immigrants in Canada is found for *every* national origin group. The Canadian assimilation rate is always smaller than the U.S. assimilation rate. In fact, the Canadian assimilation rate is sometimes insignificantly different from zero (for immigrants from Europe and Latin America).

Table 7.3   Rates of Earnings Growth and Assimilation

| | Country of destination | | | | | |
| | U.S.A. | | | Canada | | |
Origin	g_i	g_n	g_i-g_n	g_i	g_n	g_i-g_n
All Immigrants	.0277	.0186	.0091	.0238	.0198	.0040
	(39.57)	(37.00)	(10.58)	(23.80)	(66.00)	(3.83)
Africa	.0538	.0186	.0352	.0336	.0198	.0138
	(11.96)	(37.00)	(8.34)	(4.73)	(66.00)	(1.94)
Asia	.0424	.0186	.0238	.0337	.0198	.0139
	(30.29)	(37.00)	(16.01)	(10.21)	(66.00)	(4.19)
Europe	.0274	.0186	.0088	.0203	.0198	.0005
	(30.44)	(37.00)	(8.55)	(16.92)	(66.00)	(.40)
Latin America	.0222	.0186	.0036	.0223	.0198	.0025
	(22.20)	(37.00)	(3.22)	(4.85)	(66.00)	(.54)

NOTE: The t-ratios are presented in parentheses.

An additional insight provided by table 7.3 is that assimilation rates (in either country of destination) tend to be highest for immigrants originating in countries that "differ" from the host country. For example, immigrants from Africa and Asia tend to have relatively high rates of earnings growth in both Canada and the U.S. This result is not altogether surprising since it is precisely these types of immigrants who have the most to gain from accumulating "new" types of labor market experience.

A third set of summary statistics that can be calculated from the regressions estimating equations (13) and (14) is the level of the entry wage of each particular cohort, relative to "similar" natives. This entry wage was defined in chapter 4 and predicts the wage differential between immigrants and natives at age 20, at the time both groups enter the labor market. Table 7.4 presents the entry wage calculated in both the U.S. and Canadian samples (as well as predicted entry wages calculated for Australia, which will be discussed below). Consider first the data presented for the U.S. and Canadian samples.

The entry wage statistics presented in table 7.4, of course, reveal that a systematic decline in the relative earnings of immigrants occurred over the last 20 years in both the U.S., and in the pooled

Table 7.4 Earnings Differentials Between Immigrants and Natives at the Time of Entry

Origin and destination	Immigrant Cohort					
	1975–80	1970–74	1965–69	1960–64	1950–54	<1950
All Immigrants in:						
USA	−.4481	−.3053	−.2652	−.2278	−.2086	−.2276
	(−31.15)	(−19.91)	(−16.15)	(−12.37)	(−10.02)	(−9.07)
Canada	−.3095	−.2103	−.1247	−.1429	−.1141	−.0585
	(−15.22)	(−9.01)	(−5.47)	(−5.29)	(−3.93)	(−1.67)
Australia	−.1162	−.1176	−.1882	−.2052	−.2641	−.2225
	(−3.60)	(−5.26)	(−11.51)	(−12.67)	(−20.11)	(−11.84)
African Immigrants in:						
USA	−1.0832	−1.0150	−.8477	−.8630	−.9050	−.8858
	(−22.98)	(−15.26)	(−10.29)	(−8.55)	(−7.37)	(−5.16)
Canada	−.6864	−.7327	−.5462	−.6069	−.5367	−.0664
	(−6.15)	(−5.62)	(−4.12)	(−4.08)	(−3.22)	(−.14)
Australia	−.5471	−.5980	−.4974	−.5100	−.7196	−.8264
	(−3.28)	(−5.18)	(−5.91)	(−4.88)	(−1.85)	(−6.01)
Asian Immigrants in:						
USA	−.7453	−.6186	−.6326	−.6256	−.7312	−.7248
	(−36.91)	(−25.47)	(−23.48)	(−19.23)	(−19.34)	(−14.60)
Canada	−.6711	−.6440	−.5315	−.6433	−.6649	−.2145
	(−12.96)	(−10.37)	(−8.26)	(−8.00)	(−7.53)	(−1.36)
Australia	−.4405	−.3749	−.6120	−.6139	−.7589	−.3631
	(−5.83)	(−7.10)	(−12.37)	(−9.41)	(−14.74)	(−5.09)
European Immigrants in:						
USA	−.2829	−.1928	−.1543	−.1325	−.1454	−.1543
	(−16.11)	(−10.02)	(−7.90)	(−5.94)	(−5.80)	(−5.14)
Canada	−.0611	.0018	−.0074	−.0386	.0020	.0328
	(−2.30)	(.01)	(−.28)	(1.22)	(.01)	(.85)
Australia	−.0183	−.0579	−.1452	−.1660	−.2049	−.1761
	(−.41)	(2.21)	(7.95)	(−9.67)	(−14.89)	(−8.85)
Latin American Immigrants in:						
USA	−.3436	−.1993	−.1964	−.1562	−.2003	−.2349
	(−20.99)	(−10.98)	(−9.68)	(−6.70)	(−7.37)	(−6.50)
Canada	−.3824	−.3333	−.2206	−.1743	−.2270	.1276
	(−5.48)	(−4.15)	(−2.66)	(−1.76)	(−1.95)	(.49)
Australia	.1054	−.1294	−.4608	−.3338	.0211	−.3485
	(.45)	(−.72)	(−2.83)	(−1.41)	(.04)	(−.85)

NOTE: The t-ratios are presented in parentheses.

Canadian sample. For instance, the typical immigrant arriving in 1960-1964 started out his or her U.S. career earnings 22.8 percent less than the typical native person in that age group, but for 1975–1979 immigrants the wage disadvantage increased to 44.8 percent. Similarly, the Canadian data reveal that 1960–64 immigrants started out at a 14.3 percent wage disadvantage, while the 1975–1980 immigrants began with a 31 percent disadvantage.

Table 7.4 also documents the sizable differentials in the relative entry wage of immigrants across the various national origin groups. As suggested earlier, immigrants from Africa and Asia begin their labor market experience in either host country with a sizable wage disadvantage. On the other hand, immigrants originating in Europe perform relatively well in both the Canadian and American labor markets. In fact, in the case of Europeans who migrated to Canada in the 1965–1975 decade, there is *no* entry wage disadvantage: these European immigrants had an earnings capacity on the date of entry into Canada roughly the same as that of Canadian natives also entering the labor market.

The results in tables 7.3 and 7.4 provide an interesting interpretation of the concept of "assimilation." The summary statistics presented in these tables suggest that immigrants who have relatively low entry wages have the highest assimilation rates. In a sense, therefore, assimilation is a type of "regression towards the mean." Foreign-born persons entering the labor market with the greatest disadvantage have the most to gain from accumulating labor market experience in the host country.

As noted earlier, the Australian census is only available for 1981. Since the system of earnings functions given in equations (13) and (14) cannot be estimated in a single cross-section, the structural parameters identifying aging and cohort effects cannot be calculated directly. Recall, however, that the single cross-section regressions estimated in the Australian data (and presented in table 6.2) documented that foreign-born persons in Australia have significantly different age/earnings cross-section profiles from their counterparts in the U.S. and Canada. In particular, *in the cross-section,* there seems to be little relationship between the relative earnings of immigrants in Australia and the length of residence in Australia. If there is *any* assimilation or convergence effect, therefore, these results must imply that the quality of immigrants to Australia has increased over the sample period.

A rough estimate of this increase can be obtained if it is assumed that the unobserved assimilation or aging effect experienced by immigrants in Australia resembles the assimilation effect of similar foreign-born persons (i.e., persons from the same country of origin) in Canada or the United States. Given this approximation, the aging or assimilation effect can be subtracted from the Australian cross-section coefficients (thus netting out the role played by pure aging in the generation of the cross-section results), and the entry wages of the various immigrant cohorts to Australia can be calculated. In other words, the cross-section coefficients for Australia presented in table 6.2 can be adjusted for the amount of earnings growth that took place since the immigrant arrived, and in effect an entry wage differential between immigrants and natives is obtained.

There are, however, two sets of estimates for the assimilation effects (one for Canada and one for the U.S.). Thus a number of different estimates for the entry wage of immigrants choosing Australia as their destination can be calculated. A variety of these permutations were tried out, and all of them led to similar qualitative findings. In this monograph, therefore, the assimilation rate that will be used to net out the Australian cross-section will be the average of the two assimilation rates experienced by immigrants (by country of origin) in the United States and Canada.[1]

The predicted entry wages for Australian immigrants, relative to the wages of "similar" natives, are also presented in table 7.4. Two substantive results are worth noting. As implied by the flat earnings profiles found in the Australian cross-section, the quality of immigrants to Australia increased over the last 20–30 years. The typical immigrant entering Australia in 1960–64, for instance, had a 20.5 percent earnings disadvantage relative to natives, while the most recent immigrants earned only 11.6 percent less than comparable natives at the time of entry. Second, this increase in the quality of immigrants to Australia is documented for each of the national origin groups under analysis. For instance, Asian immigrants arriving in

Australia during the late 1970s had a 44 percent wage disadvantage at the time of entry, while the Asian immigrants arriving in Australia during the 1960s had a wage disadvantage that exceeded 60 percent. Similarly, European immigrants arriving in Australia in the late 1970s have the same wage as natives *on the date of arrival*, while European immigrants in the 1960s had wage disadvantages of about 15 percent at the time of entry.

As noted in chapter 1, much of the early literature analyzing the earnings of immigrants dealt with the concept and measurements of "overtaking," the age at which the earnings of immigrants reach parity with and overtake the earnings of natives. An alternative (and conceptually better) way of measuring the life-cycle wealth of immigrants is provided by equation (17), which shows how information on entry wages and on average growth rates of both immigrant and native wages can be combined to calculate the present value differential between immigrant cohorts and natives. These calculated present value differentials are presented in table 7.5, where it must be cautioned again that the Australian estimates are quite rough since only one Australian census is available. As noted earlier, the present value calculations provide a measure of the labor market performance of immigrants and natives over the entire life cycle, and is therefore the best available measure of how immigrants do in the labor market.

The results presented in table 7.5 are quite interesting. For instance, the typical immigrant arriving in the United States in 1960–1964 had only a slight earnings disadvantage relative to a comparable native over the entire life cycle, while the most recent immigrant arriving in the United States (the post-1975 cohort) has a wage disadvantage of nearly 27 percent over the life cycle. Thus, recent immigrants will have accumulated substantially lower levels of "wealth" over the life cycle than comparable natives. Table 7.5 also illustrates the now familiar result that the Canadian census reveals a roughly similar pattern for the sample of pooled immigrants: the 1960–1964 cohort of immigrants in Canada has a 6 percent wage disadvantage (relative to natives) over the entire life cycle, but the disadvantage increases to 23 percent for the most recent cohort of Canadian immigrants.

Table 7.5   Present Value Differentials Between Immigrants and Natives

Group	Year of arrival					
	1975–80	1970–74	1965–69	1960–64	1950–54	<1950
All Immigrants in:						
USA	−.2656	−.1228	−.0827	−.0453	−.0260	−.0451
	(−18.99)	(−12.20)	(−10.40)	(−6.88)	(−4.37)	(−4.38)
Canada	−.2297	−.1306	−.0449	−.0632	−.0344	.0212
	(−13.25)	(−8.57)	(−3.75)	(−4.63)	(−3.57)	(1.10)
Australia	.0149	.0136	−.0570	−.0740	−.1330	−.0914
	(.46)	(.61)	(−3.49)	(−4.57)	(−10.12)	(−4.86)
African Immigrants in:						
USA	−.3779	−.3097	−.1425	−.1577	−.1997	−.1806
	(−5.11)	(−6.08)	(−3.21)	(−3.62)	(−4.28)	(−1.69)
Canada	−.4092	−.4555	−.2690	−.3297	−.2595	.2108
	(−3.00)	(−3.23)	(−2.03)	(−2.55)	(−2.65)	(.61)
Australia	−.1688	−.2197	−.1191	−.1317	−.3413	−.4481
	(−1.01)	(−1.90)	(−1.42)	(−1.26)	(−.88)	(−3.26)
Asian Immigrants in:						
USA	−.2692	−.4117	−.1565	−.1495	−.2551	−.2487
	(−11.47)	(−8.33)	(−10.53)	(−9.89)	(−17.54)	(−9.08)
Canada	−.3930	−.3658	−.2534	−.3651	−.3868	.0637
	(−6.88)	(−6.56)	(−4.86)	(−6.38)	(−10.19)	(.54)
Australia	−.0634	.0022	−.2348	−.2367	−.3817	.0141
	(−.84)	(.04)	(−4.75)	(−3.63)	(−7.42)	(.20)
European Immigrants in:						
USA	−.1068	−.0167	.0218	.0436	.0307	.0219
	(−6.06)	(−1.25)	(2.14)	(5.07)	(4.44)	(1.79)
Canada	−.0516	.0113	.0022	−.0290	.0116	.0423
	(−2.22)	(.55)	(.14)	(−1.92)	(1.04)	(2.04)
Australia	.0745	.0350	−.0524	−.0732	−.1121	−.0833
	(1.68)	(1.33)	(−2.87)	(−4.26)	(−8.15)	(−4.18)
Latin American Immigrants in:						
USA	−.2716	−.1273	−.1243	−.0841	−.1282	−.1629
	(−14.62)	(−9.53)	(−11.42)	(−8.91)	(−13.56)	(−8.18)
Canada	−.3312	−.2820	−.1693	−.1230	−.1757	.1788
	(−3.77)	(−3.25)	(−2.10)	(−1.46)	(−3.07)	(.91)
Australia	.1671	−.0677	−.3991	−.2721	.0827	−.2868
	(.61)	(−.38)	(−2.45)	(−1.15)	(.15)	(−.70)

NOTE: The t-ratios are presented in parentheses.

The present value differentials presented in table 7.5 also document the fact that there exist substantial differences in labor market performance across immigrants from different countries of origin. European immigrants in both Canada and the United States have life-cycle earnings streams which are approximately similar to those of comparable natives. For instance, European individuals who migrated in the 1970–1974 period to either Canada or the United States have life-cycle earnings streams which are basically identical to those of natives in each of the two host countries. On the other hand, immigrants originating in Asia perform quite badly in both the American and Canadian labor market: Asians who migrated in 1970–74 have about 40 percent lower earnings (calculated over the entire life cycle) than comparable natives.

The present value differentials calculated for Australia reveal that the typical person migrating to Australia in the late 1970s had essentially the same present value of earnings over the life cycle as comparable natives, while immigrants arriving in Australia in the 1960s had a 6–7 percent wage disadvantage. As in Canada and the United States, Europeans migrating to Australia generally tend to have the highest present value of earnings (relative to natives), while those originating in Africa or Asia tend to have the greatest disadvantage. For instance, the most recent European migrants will accumulate about 7.5 percent higher earnings than natives over the life cycle, while those originating in Africa will accumulate 17 percent lower earnings than natives.

In addition to these substantive results, the data presented in table 7.5 provides a unique descriptive analysis of an important question in immigration policy. Given that there exists an immigration market which sorts the pool of potential emigrants across competing host countries, who are the "winners" and the "losers" in this international marketplace? Table 7.5 provides important insights into this problem if it is assumed that the native-base across the three host countries has a similar level of productivity and skills. This assumption makes the *relative* wage of immigrants (i.e., the difference between the immigrant wage and the wage of comparable natives) across host countries directly comparable as an index of immigrant quality. The assumption that natives among the three host countries are roughly similar in terms of skills and productivity, of course, is not empirically verifiable. However, it does not seem unreasonable since Australia, Canada, and the United States all share a common language, culture, political and economic systems, and are at similar stages of economic development.

Given this assumption, the statistics presented in table 7.5 provide an interesting story of the extent of self-selection in the generation of the foreign-born population in each of the host countries. This story is best told by figures 7.1 and 7.2 which present graphically the data summarized in table 7.5. Consider initially figure 7.1, which represents the trends in the relative present values of earnings calculated for the pooled immigrant sample in table 7.5. Prior to 1960–1965, Australia attracted immigrants who performed much worse (over the life cycle) than immigrants attracted by Canada or the United States. This type of selection, however, changed drastically by the 1970s. During the 1970–1980 decade, Australia began attracting immigrants who had the highest present values of earnings, and the United States began to attract

FIGURE 7.1

Relative Wage of Immigrant Cohorts in the Host Countries

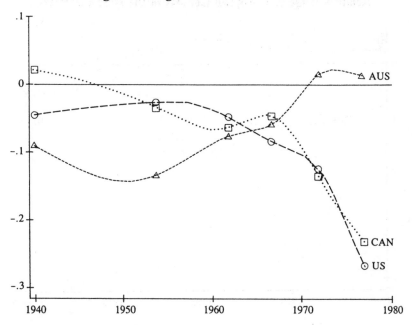

FIGURE 7.2

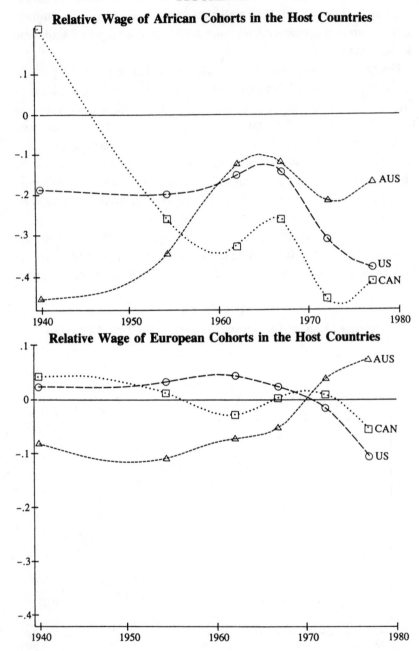

Relative Wage of African Cohorts in the Host Countries

Relative Wage of European Cohorts in the Host Countries

Relative Wage of Asian Cohorts in the Host Countries

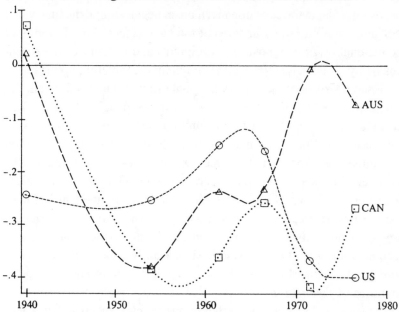

Relative Wage of Latin American Cohorts in the Host Countries

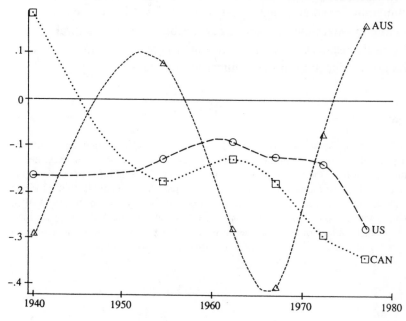

persons who had the lowest present values of earnings. It is noteworthy that the reversal in the selection mechanism began around the time when U.S. immigration policy underwent radical changes, both in terms of the national origin composition of migrants and in terms of the mechanisms by which visas were allocated among competing applicants.

The comparison of the data by national origin groups leads to similar conclusions, and is illustrated in the various panels of figure 7.2. Consider, for example, European immigrants. Those choosing Australia prior to 1960–1964 had substantially lower earnings capacities than those choosing Canada or the United States. By the late 1970s, however, Europeans choosing Australia had the highest present values of earnings (relative to natives) while those choosing the United States had the lowest present values of earnings. Exactly the same patterns can be found in the sample of Asian immigrants, where the earnings accumulation over the life cycle is significantly greater for Australian immigrants in the 1970s than for Asian immigrants choosing other countries of destination.

The statistical analysis presented in this chapter, therefore, reveals a fundamental shift in the ''competitiveness'' of the United States in the immigration market over the last two decades. The next chapter will attempt to determine the factors responsible for this structural shift in the mechanism which sorts the potential pool of migrants across the countries competing in the immigration market.

NOTES

[1]The assimilation rate used to net out the aging effect from the Australian cross-section wage differentials is *not* the average annual rate of growth presented in table 7.3. Instead, the rate of growth of men aged 20–25 is used to net out the aging effect for the most recent cohort (who are, on average, 23 years old in 1980); the rate of growth of men aged 25–30 is used to net out the aging effect for the 1970–1974 cohort (who are, on average 28 years old in 1980), etc. This methodology, therefore, ensures that nonlinearities in the age/earnings profile are accounted for in netting out the aging effects from the Australian cross-section earnings profile.

8

Determinants of Immigrant Sorting Across Host Countries

The summary statistics presented in table 7.5 document the fact that there are both country-of-origin and country-of-destination effects on the relative earnings of immigrants. In other words, characteristics of both the countries where immigrants come from and the countries where immigrants go to determine how foreign-born persons perform in the labor market of the host country. An important question is raised by this interesting empirical result: can the differences documented in table 7.5 be explained in terms of the observable characteristics of the countries of origin and destination?

If potential migrants are wealth-maximizers, the theoretical discussion in chapter 3 suggests that the "quality" of immigrants (i.e., the earnings of immigrants relative to the earnings of comparable natives) will be determined by such factors as the extent of income inequality in both the origin and destination countries, the types of policies that regulate migration flows across countries, and the types of skills that immigrants carry with them into their destination. This type of model, therefore, implies the existence of a "quality-of-immigrants" equation given by:

$$r_{ij}(t) = X_i(t)\alpha + Z_j(t)\beta + \epsilon_{ij}(t) \qquad (22)$$

where $r_{ij}(t)$ is the relative wage (in the host country) of a cohort migrating from country i to country j at time t; $X_i(t)$ is a vector of variables describing conditions in the country of origin i at time t; and $Z_j(t)$ is a vector of variables describing conditions in the country of destination j at time t. Equation (22) succinctly summarizes the hypothesis that the relative performance of immigrants in the host country's labor market (i.e., the statistics presented in table 7.5) are determined by both country-of-origin and country-of-destination characteristics.

There is one crucial technical property implicit in equation (22) that deserves careful discussion. The relative earnings of immigrants from country i to country j at time t are independent of events in other time periods t' ($t' = t$); more important, the relative earnings are also independent of conditions in other countries (in particular, they are independent of conditions in other potential countries of destination). Although this assumption is not likely to be strictly satisfied (after all, economic and political conditions in alternative host countries determine the size and directions of migration flows), it does simplify the empirical analysis presented in this chapter substantially. If the assumption were invalid, for instance, the right-hand side of equation (22) would have to be expanded to include the characteristics of all other potential countries of destination, and the increase in the number of variables would rapidly drive the number of degrees of freedom to zero, thus preventing the estimation of the model.

In order to have well-defined immigrant cohorts, the analysis is restricted to the present value differentials of the four cohorts that migrated after 1960 (i.e., the 1960–64, 1965–69, 1970–74 and post-1975 cohorts). The calendar year of migration is reported in slightly different ways by the Censuses in the various host countries. The restriction of the analysis in this chapter to the last four cohorts ensures that differences in definitions do not play an important role in the generation of the empirical results. Since there are four cohorts, four regions of origin (i.e., Africa, Asia, Europe, and Latin America), and three countries of destination, equation (22) is estimated on a sample of 48 observations. The dependent variable is obtained from the present value differences for these 48 observations reported in table 7.5.

Table 8.1 presents the estimated regression and defines the independent variables used to proxy for the characteristics of the countries of origin and the countries of destination. The explanatory variables include the percentage difference between the GNP per capita in the country of origin and the GNP per capita in the country of destination as of the time of migration. Table 8.1 shows that this variable has an

Table 8.1   Determinants of Immigrant Quality Across Host Countries

Variable	Coefficient	t
CONSTANT	.1252	(−2.77)
USLAW	−.0511	(−1.79)
UNEMPLOYMENT	.0011	(.18)
INEQUALITY(0)	−.0044	(−1.89)
INEQUALITY(1)	.0431	(4.35)
ΔGNP	.0903	(8.78)
R^2	.801	

Key to Variables: USLAW = 1 if cohort migrated to U.S. in 1970–1980; UNEMPLOYMENT = unemployment rate in the host country at the time of migration; INEQUALITY(0) = average income inequality in selected countries from the continent of origin in the decade of migration; INEQUALITY(1) = inequality measure for destination countries in the decade of migration; ΔGNP = percentage difference in GNP per capita between sending and host countries at time of migration.

important (both numerically and statistically) positive impact on the relative earnings of immigrants. The larger the GNP per capita in the country of origin relative to the GNP per capita in the country of destination, the better the labor market performance of immigrants in the host country. This finding, of course, simply restates the observation in chapter 7 that immigrants originating in European countries tend to perform much better in any of the three host countries than immigrants originating in other continents. The result is probably caused by the fact that the labor markets in Europe and in each of the three host countries greatly resemble each other (they are, for the most part, technologically advanced economies). These skills are carried by the migration flows across international boundaries and are rewarded in the host countries.

An additional variable in table 8.1 is the unemployment rate in the country of destination. This variable, though positive, does not have a significant impact on the relative earnings of immigrants. The very weak positive effect suggests that when the unemployment rate is high, the types of immigrants most likely to be affected by the deteriorating labor market conditions (namely, unskilled persons) are least likely to emigrate. Hence the average productivity of the pool of persons that *does* migrate increases.

Table 8.1 also includes variables measuring the extent of income inequality in the countries of origin and in the countries of destination.[1] Both of these variables have a statistically significant impact on the relative earnings of immigrants, and they behave exactly as predicted by the theoretical framework in chapter 3. In particular, migrants originating in countries where income inequality is very high do substantially worse in the host country than other migrants. This result can be understood by noting that as income inequality in the country of origin increases, the economic welfare of the least unskilled persons deteriorates significantly (thus increasing their incentives to migrate), while the economic welfare of the most skilled persons improves (thus decreasing their incentives to migrate). The self-selected immigrant flow out of countries where income inequality is large, therefore, will tend to be composed mainly of unskilled persons. This is precisely what the regression in table 8.1 indicates.

In addition, the regression shows that the greater the extent of income inequality in the host country, the better the labor market performance of immigrants. This result can also be understood in the context of the wealth-maximization framework. In particular, the greater the extent of income inequality in the host country, the greater the incentives for skilled persons to migrate (since ability is highly rewarded in countries with high levels of income inequality), and the lower the incentives for unskilled persons to migrate (since the high level of income inequality in the host country implies that they will not perform relatively well in the labor market). Hence the self-selected migration flow will be composed mainly of skilled persons.

Finally, the regression in table 8.1 includes a variable designed to capture the impact of the change in U.S. immigration policy on the quality of the flow of migrants choosing the United States as their destination. This effect is captured by a dummy variable set to unity if the immigrant cohort chose the U.S. in the post-1970 period, and zero otherwise.[2] Table 8.1 shows that the impact of this variable on the relative earnings of immigrants is negative and significant. In other words, the post-1965 change in U.S. immigration policy (which became effective in 1968) led to migration flows that performed significantly worse in the U.S. labor market than earlier waves. The regression presented in table 8.1 suggests that, holding all other factors constant, post-1970 cohorts of immigrants in the U.S. have about 5 percent lower earnings potential over their life cycle than pre-1970 cohorts of immigrants in the U.S.

The analysis summarized by the regression in table 8.1, therefore, indicates that the sorting of immigrants across the three host countries is not a random process. Instead the observed differences in the relative earnings of immigrants across the host countries can be understood within a systematic, economic framework. The composition of the migrant flows from the countries of origin to Australia, Canada, and the United States is heavily influenced by both economic variables and by the changes in immigration policy that occurred during the period (particularly in the United States). The sorting of persons across countries carried out by the immigration market, therefore, is an example of a well-behaved economic system, where individuals migrate to the countries where they are likely to be the most productive, given the constraints imposed by the economic conditions of the host countries and by the institutional framework of immigration policy.

NOTES

[1]The inequality measure is the ratio of income accruing to the top 10 percent of the households to the income accruing to the bottom 20 percent of the households. Since these data are not available by continent, the values assigned to each continent reflect the average value of the variable across the three or four countries in each continent which form the bulk of the migration flows.

[2]Since the 1965 Amendments to the Immigration and Nationality Act did not become fully effective until 1968, the 1970–74 and 1975–79 cohorts are the only groups whose migration was entirely regulated by the Amendments.

9

Labor Flows Between Canada and the United States

The empirical analysis presented in the previous chapter studies the labor market performance of the migration flows into the three host countries. Since little is known about the persons who did not emigrate (i.e., the population of persons who decided to remain in their countries of origin), no comparisons can be made between the pool of migrants and the population of "stayers." Of course, such a comparison could be made if censuses were available in the various countries of origin so that the composition of the pool of persons who decided to remain in that country could be determined. The empirical analysis presented in the previous chapters, therefore, looks only at the side of the immigration market observable in census data of the host countries (how immigrants perform in their chosen country of residence), and ignores the side of the immigration market that is unobservable (how immigrants compare to the population of persons who decided not to migrate).

Fortunately, however, such an analysis can be conducted for the migration flows between Canada and the United States. These migration flows have long interested demographers (see, for example, Boyd 1976; and Lavoie 1972). As will be seen below, large numbers of persons born in the United States emigrate to Canada, and large numbers of persons born in Canada emigrate to the United States. The availability of micro census data in 1970–1971 and in 1980–1981 for both countries implies that the labor market performance of U.S. emigrants can be compared to that of U.S. natives who decided not to migrate, and that the earnings of Canadian immigrants in the United States can be compared to the earnings of Canadians who remained in Canada. This type of analysis thus allows a significant expansion of the

Table 9.1   Foreign-Born Populations in Canada and the United States* (1980/1981)

	Canada	United States
Population (in 1000's)	24,343.0	226,545.8
Foreign-Born:		
Total	3,874.2	14,079.9
Born in Canada	—	842.9
Born in U.S.	315.9	—
Percent of population foreign-born:	15.9	6.2
Percent of immigrants born in:		
Canada	—	6.0
U.S.	8.2	—

NOTE: *The Canadian statistics refer to 1981, while the U.S. statistics refer to 1980.
SOURCES: U.S. Department of Commerce (1986) and the 1981 Canadian Census Public Use Sample.

focus of empirical research in the immigration literature. Rather than simply measure how the foreign-born compare to the native-born in any given host country (the question that has motivated practically all research in the last decade), the joint study of the U.S. and Canadian censuses allows the analysis of such questions as: (1) Which kinds of persons emigrate the United States? (2) How well do they do in their chosen country of residence (i.e., Canada)? (3) Do the same selection biases characterize both the American and Canadian transnational flows?

The numerical importance of the labor flows between the United States and Canada is documented in table 9.1, which presents counts of foreign-born persons in each of the two countries in 1980–1981. The 1980 U.S. census enumerated over 14 million foreign-born persons in the country, or slightly over 6 percent of the U.S. population. The 1981 Canadian census enumerated 3.9 million immigrants, or almost 16 percent of the Canadian population. In 1980–1981, nearly 850 thousand persons born in Canada resided in the U.S., and over 300 thousand persons born in the U.S. resided in Canada. U.S. emigration to Canada, therefore, accounts for 8 percent of the foreign-born population in Canada, while Canadian emigration to the United States accounts for 6 percent of the foreign-born population in the U.S. Transnational migration flows across the two

Table 9.2   Aggregate Economic Indicators for U.S. and Canada

	1970		1980	
	U.S.	Canada	U.S.	Canada
Per capita gross domestic product (in dollars)	4826	4371	11446	11479
Labor force participation rate:				
Male	85.4	85.7	84.3	86.3
Female	48.9	43.2	59.7	57.2
Unemployment rate	4.9	5.7	7.1	7.5

SOURCE: U.S. Department of Commerce (1986).

countries, therefore, are sizable, and a study of the labor market outcomes experienced by the various groups of "movers" and "stayers" may reveal important insights into the process of self-selection that determines the migration decision.

The kinds of insights that the study of the transnational flows can yield are easily seen if it is assumed that the average person born in Canada has essentially the same productivity level (or "quality") as the average person born in the United States. This assumption, though it cannot be empirically verified, does not seem unreasonable in light of the similar economic and cultural characteristics of the two countries. Table 9.2 documents the similarity in key aggregate economic characteristics between the U.S. and Canadian economies in the 1970–1980 period. The per capita gross domestic product in 1980, for example, differed by only $33 between the two countries; the labor force participation rates of both men and women were basically the same in the two countries; and the aggregate 1980 unemployment rate was 7.1 percent in the U.S. and 7.5 percent in Canada.

This strong similarity in key economic characteristics suggests that the assumption of equal productivity across the two native populations is empirically justified. Given this hypothesis, the *relative* earnings of Canadians in the United States (i.e., the earnings of Canadian immigrants relative to the earnings of native Americans with the same socioeconomic characteristics) can be used to infer how the Canadian immigrants performed in Canada prior to their emigration. Similarly, the *relative* earnings of Americans in Canada (relative to the average

Table 9.3 Summary Characteristics

	United States					
	Natives		Canadian immigrants		British immigrants	
Variable	1970	1980	1970	1980	1970	1980
ln (wage rate)	1.37	2.04	1.51	2.19	1.57	2.28
Education	11.5	12.7	11.5	12.9	12.5	14.1
Age	42.1	40.7	46.6	45.2	45.9	43.7
Y75	—	—	—	.09	—	.19
Y70	—	—	—	.05	—	.08
Y65	—	—	.10	.10	.18	.14
Y60	—	—	.11	.15	.14	.13
Y50	—	—	.21	.29	.23	.26
Y40	—	—	.58	.32	.44	.20
Sample Size	28978	15071	3420	7083	2231	5475

	Canada					
	Natives		American immigrants		British immigrants	
Variable	1971	1981	1971	1981	1971	1981
ln (wage rate)	1.28	2.24	1.45	2.34	1.42	2.41
Education	9.9	11.3	12.6	14.5	11.8	12.8
Age	41.0	39.5	44.6	42.6	44.5	43.6
Y75	—	—	—	.14	—	.11
Y70	—	—	—	.18	—	.08
Y65	—	—	.26	.22	.18	.17
Y60	—	—	.09	.07	.07	.10
Y50	—	—	.15	.18	.47	.47
Y40	—	—	.49	.22	.28	.08
Sample Size	28049	61205	511	924	2079	3729

native Canadian of comparable socioeconomic characteristics) provide substantive information about how American emigrants would have performed in the United States. Hence, the joint study of transnational migration flows across the Canadian/American border provides a valuable and unique opportunity to analyze how a country's emigrants compare to the country's population that chose not to emigrate!

Table 9.3 presents the means of the variables for the samples of

American and Canadian natives, and for the samples of transnational migrants. In addition, to provide some comparability, the summary statistics of the sample of migrants originating in the United Kingdom are also presented. The sample of British immigrants is chosen because this group of persons also originates in an English-speaking country and may closely resemble the transnational migrants. Finally, since the analysis in this chapter is restricted to the U.S. and Canadian censuses, the dependent variable is the logarithm of the wage rate in the year prior to the Census.

The statistics presented in table 9.3 yield several interesting facts. For instance, Canadian immigrants in the United States do quite well in the labor market. In both the 1970 and 1980 censuses, they report wage rates substantially above the wages reported by the native population. It is remarkable that these high wage rates cannot be attributed to higher education levels among Canadian immigrants in the U.S. The education levels of Canadian immigrants and U.S. natives are essentially identical, but the immigrants earned about 15 percent more than the natives in 1980.

Table 9.3 also shows that, as suggested by the changes in U.S. immigration policy (which in the post-1965 period numerically restrict the number of Canadians who can be legally admitted into the United States), the average Canadian immigrant in the U.S. has resided in the U.S. far longer than the typical immigrant. Over 60 percent of all Canadian immigrants in the 1980 census, for example, arrived in the United States prior to 1960, while the respective statistic for the sample of pooled immigrants is 32 percent.

The summary statistics in the Canadian census also provide interesting insights. The average American in Canada earns about 10 percent more than the typical native. This difference, however, can probably be accounted for by the fact that the average American in Canada has a much higher level of education than all other groups under analysis. The average American in Canada has a 10 percent higher wage rate than the average Canadian native and has about three more years of schooling than the average native in either Canada or the United States.

The comparisons of the characteristics (particularly educational) of the transnational migrants with the "stayers" yields one important result. Both Canada and the United States are exporting and importing highly educated persons. The transnational migration flow can, therefore, be characterized as a two-way brain drain in terms of educational background. The reasons for this type of immigrant self-selection in terms of education will be discussed below. The average American immigrant in Canada, however, does not seem to be doing exceptionally well given his education. On the other hand, the average Canadian immigrant in the United States has a relatively high wage rate and appears to be quite successful. The selection mechanism generating the transnational flows in each of the two countries, therefore, seem to differ significantly in terms of unobserved characteristics, with Canada exporting and the United States importing individuals with high levels of ability or unobserved skills.

Within each host country, the samples of natives and of transnational migrants are used to estimate the earnings functions in (13) and (14). The regressions are presented in table 9.4. The effects of some of the independent variables in these regressions are of interest. In particular, consider the impact of education on the native wage structures in each host country. The return to an additional year of schooling is about 5.6 percent in the United States, and 4.4 percent in Canada. According to the theoretical framework presented in chapter 3, this differential suggests that Canada should export highly-educated persons to the United States, and that the United States should export persons with lower levels of education to Canada. In other words, if individuals are wealth-maximizers, persons will move to markets where their characteristics are valued at the highest price. The summary statistics in table 9.4, however, clearly contradict this prediction. The fact that the transnational labor flows are composed of highly educated persons in both directions is probably due to the fact that migration costs (such as information about job market opportunities) decline with educated. It is well known in the migration literature (Schwartz 1968) that internal migration flows are characterized primarily by the movement of persons with relatively high education levels.

The regressions in table 9.4 also show that the coefficients of the

Table 9.4 Earnings Functions for Natives and Transnational Immigrants (Dependent Variable = ln Wage Rate)

Variable	U.S. census		Canadian census	
	Coefficient	t	Coefficient	t
Natives :				
CONSTANT	−.7133	(−16.89)	−.6215	(−21.34)
EDUC	.0557	(68.96)	.0437	(84.15)
AGE	.0491	(24.50)	.0564	(40.33)
AGE^2	−.0005	(−20.77)	−.0006	(−35.97)
MAR	.1767	(25.07)	.1747	(37.25)
HLTH	−.0774	(−7.73)	—	—
SMSA	.2128	(37.52)	.0944	(24.45)
Transnational immigrants:				
CONSTANT	−.9760	(−10.65)	−1.5460	(−6.36)
EDUC	.0487	(31.30)	.0415	(10.70)
AGE	.0718	(17.39)	.0990	(8.57)
AGE^2	−.0007	(−15.53)	−.0010	(−8.07)
MAR	.1893	(13.03)	.1034	(2.72)
HLTH	−.1524	(−6.80)	—	—
SMSA	.1615	(12.47)	.1277	(4.08)
YSM	.0046	(1.73)	−.0392	(−5.90)
YSM^2	−.0001	(−1.62)	.0008	(5.52)
Y70	−.0910	(−2.40)	.2101	(3.14)
Y65	−.0237	(−.75)	.2849	(4.79)
Y60	−.0681	(−1.84)	.3881	(4.80)
Y50	−.0974	(−2.24)	.5347	(5.71)
Y40	−.1361	(−2.55)	.4307	(3.32)
Period Effect	.6141	(114.63)	.9458	(229.22)

Key to Variables: EDUC = years of completed schooling; MAR = 1 if married, spouse present; HLTH = 1 if health limits work; SMSA = 1 if resident of metropolitan area; YSM = years since migration; Y70 = 1 if migrated in 1970–74; Y65 = 1 if migrated in 1965–69; Y60 = 1 if migrated in 1960–64; Y50 = 1 if migrated in 1950–59; Y40 = 1 if migrated prior to 1950; and the period effect is captured by a dummy variable set to unity if the observation was drawn from the 1980/81 Census.

education variable are not all that different between the natives and the transnational migrants *within* each of the host countries. This result differs dramatically from that reported earlier where the return to a year of schooling of foreign-born men is lower than the return to native schooling in all host countries. The finding that the education of transnational migrants is highly valued in both Canada and the

United States is probably due to the fact that the educational system of the two countries (and the language) is quite similar, and hence there is very little "specificity" in the schooling of the transnational migrants.

The coefficients of the vector indicating the calendar year in which the migrant arrived (Y70, Y65, etc., where the omitted dummy variable signals post-1975 migrants) estimate the cohort effects in the transnational labor flows. The vector of these dummy variables is significant in both earnings functions. In the United States, the F statistic testing for joint significance of the variables in the vector is 2.4, while in Canada the F statistic is 8.3 (and both of these statistics are significant at the 5 percent confidence level). More important, however, is the fact that the trends in cohort quality indicated by these vectors differ so radically between Canada and the United States. The cohort coefficients in the United States suggest that the unobserved skills of the most recent Canadian immigrants are substantially *higher* than the unobserved skills of earlier Canadian immigrants. The Canadian census, on the other hand, suggests that the quality of the most recent American immigrants is substantially *lower* than the quality of the earlier American waves. For example, the most recent (i.e., post-1975) cohort of Canadian immigrants in the U.S. has a 9.1 percent higher earnings capacity than the 1970–1974 cohort, while the most recent cohort of American immigrants in Canada has 21.0 percent lower earnings than the 1970–1974 cohorts.

It is important to stress that the cohort effects documented for the transnational migrants in each of the host countries differ substantially from the cohort effects exhibited by other immigrant groups in both Canada and the United States. Recall that the statistics presented in chapter 7 revealed that the quality of most immigrant cohorts entering the United States had declined over the same period, while the trends in the quality of immigrant cohorts entering Canada depended on the country of origin. Table 9.5 presents the immigrant earnings functions from the regressions estimated in the sample of British immigrants. The trends in the cohort quality of British immigrants differ between the two host countries. The most recent British migrants arriving in the United States have somewhat higher earnings than the earlier waves

Table 9.5 Earnings Functions for Other Immigrants

| | U.S. census | | Canadian census | |
| | British immigrants in U.S. | | British immigrants in Canada | |
Variable	Coeff.	t	Coeff.	t
CONSTANT	−1.3096	(−12.04)	−.5609	(−4.59)
EDUC	.0489	(23.76)	.0429	(19.24)
AGE	.0888	(17.64)	.0539	(9.46)
AGE^2	−.0009	(−15.81)	−.0006	(−8.86)
MAR	.1952	(11.77)	.1642	(8.20)
HLTH	−.1702	(−5.39)	—	—
SMSA	.0984	(5.56)	.0738	(4.37)
YSM	.0025	(.92)	.0026	(.65)
YSM^2	−.00001	(−.34)	.00005	(.50)
Y70	−.0109	(−.32)	.0045	(.11)
Y65	−.0049	(−.18)	.0367	(1.05)
Y60	−.0522	(−1.47)	.0329	(.74)
Y50	−.0843	(−1.97)	.0040	(.09)
Y40	−.1336	(−2.38)	−.0392	(−.65)

NOTE: Regressions were jointly estimated with the native earnings functions and the restriction that the period effects are the same in the two groups was imposed.

(particularly pre-1960) of British immigrants, while there are essentially no cohort effects among British immigrants choosing Canada as their destination.

The empirical framework presented earlier showed that the estimated earnings functions can be used to calculate measures of the wage differentials between the various immigrant cohorts and natives. As before, it is assumed that the average age at migration is 20. Given this assumption, and the means of the various socioeconomic characteristics in the 1980/1981 cross-section for each of the respective immigrant groups, the regressions were used to predict the relative wages of immigrants.

Table 9.6 presents the wage differentials between immigrants and natives at the time of entry into the labor market. The most recent Canadian immigrants in the U.S. enter the labor market with essentially the same wage as comparable natives, while the most recent American immigrants in Canada enter the labor market with a 32.7

Table 9.6 Predicted Wage Differentials Between Immigrants and Natives at Time of Migration

Group	Year of immigration					
	1975–80	1970–74	1965–69	1960–64	1950–59	<1950
Canadian immigrants in U.S.	−.0272	−.1183	−.0510	−.0953	−.1246	−.1633
	(−.81)	(−2.78)	(−1.37)	(−2.22)	(−2.52)	(−4.99)
American immigrants in Canada	−.3274	−.1172	−.0425	.0608	.2074	.1033
	(−4.06)	(−1.34)	(−.52)	(.59)	(1.81)	(.70)
British immigrants in U.S.	−.1501	−.1610	−.1550	−.2023	−.2345	−.2837
	(−4.41)	(−3.70)	(−3.88)	(−4.33)	(−4.47)	(−7.49)
British immigrants in Canada	−.0175	−.0129	.0192	.0155	−.0135	−.0567
	(−.41)	(−.26)	(.42)	(.28)	(−.22)	(−.85)

NOTE: The t-ratios are presented in parentheses.

percent wage disadvantage (relative to comparable Canadian natives). Moreover, as revealed by the cohort effects estimated in table 9.4, these entry wage differentials differ significantly across cohorts. For instance, the 1950-1959 cohort of Canadian immigrants in the U.S. entered the labor market with a wage disadvantage of 12.5 percent, while the 1950-1959 cohort of American immigrants in Canada entered the labor market with a wage *advantage* of 20.7 percent over comparable natives. In terms of entry wages, therefore, the earlier waves of American immigrants in Canada outperformed comparable natives, while the earlier waves of Canadian immigrants in the U.S. were not as productive as natives.

Table 9.6 also presents entry wage differentials calculated for the various cohorts of British migrants in each of the two host countries. The statistics document significant differences in the labor market performance between the transnational migrants and the British immigrants in each of the host countries. For example, even though recent Canadian immigrants in the U.S. begin their labor market career with the same wage as American natives, the most recent British immigrants begin their U.S. working life cycle with a 15 percent wage disadvantage. Similarly, even though the most recent wave of American immigrants in Canada has relatively low entry wages, the most recent wave of British immigrants in Canada earn about the same as comparable Canadian natives.

The unsuccessful labor market performance of American immigrants in Canada is also revealed by the estimates of the assimilation rate of the various immigrant cohorts. Recall that $g_i(g_n)$ was defined as the average rate of growth of immigrant (native) earnings in the first 30 years of the working life cycle. The estimated rates of assimilation are presented in table 9.7. These statistics show that, if anything, Canadian immigrants in the U.S. have a *higher* rate of assimilation than other immigrants, and that American immigrants in Canada have a *lower* rate of assimilation than other immigrants. These results provide striking evidence that the assimilation rates presented in table 9.7 are not simply measuring a "regression towards the mean" in immigrant earnings. After all, it would not be surprising to find that immigrants who have relatively low entry wages exhibit the highest

Table 9.7 Average Rates of Growth in Immigrant and Native Earnings

Group	g_i	g_n	g_i-g_n
Canadian immigrants	.0243	.0154	.0089
in U.S.	(12.78)	(30.80)	(4.58)
American immigrants	.0101	.0152	−.0051
in Canada	(2.35)	(50.67)	(−1.18)
British immigrants	.0283	.0154	.0129
in U.S.	(14.15)	(30.80)	(6.32)
British immigrants	.0180	.0152	.0028
in Canada	(8.57)	(50.67)	(1.32)

NOTE: The t-ratios are presented in parentheses.

rates of "catch-up." This expectation, however, is not confirmed by the estimated assimilation rates. The relatively high-quality Canadian immigrants in the U.S., who have very high entry wages, also have a very steep age/earnings profile (compared to the typical immigrant in the U.S.). Conversely, the relatively low-quality American immigrant in Canada, who has *lower* entry wages than the typical immigrant in Canada, actually has a negative rate of convergence, so that the economic position of this cohort, if anything, deteriorates over time.

Equation (17) shows that the entry wages and the assimilation rates can be combined to calculate the difference in the present values of the immigrant and native age/earnings profiles. These calculations are presented in table 9.8 for the various cohorts under analysis. These summary measures of wealth strikingly show the extent to which American immigrants in Canada differ from other immigrant groups. For example, even though the most recent Canadian arriving in the United States has a present value of earnings 15 percent higher than the comparable native, the most recent American arriving in Canada has a present value of earnings 43 percent below that of comparable natives. These statistics, in fact, are extreme values in table 9.8. No other immigrant group being analyzed (in the post-1975 cohort) does as well as Canadian immigrants in the United States, and no other immigrant group being analyzed (in the post-1975 cohort) does as badly as American immigrants in Canada.

These results have important implications for the question of which

Table 9.8 Predicted Present Value Differentials Between Immigrants and Natives

	Year of immigration					
Group	1975–80	1970–74	1965–69	1960–64	1950–59	<1950
Canadian immigrants	.1511	.0600	.1273	.0830	.0537	.0150
in U.S.	(4.24)	(1.80)	(5.79)	(5.12)	(8.75)	(.61)
American immigrants	−.4301	−.2200	−.1452	−.0419	.1046	.0006
in Canada	(−5.98)	(−3.75)	(−2.96)	(−.70)	(2.42)	(.01)
British immigrants	.1079	.0970	.1030	.0557	.0235	.0257
in U.S.	(3.16)	(3.04)	(4.52)	(2.84)	(1.40)	(.86)
British immigrants	.0376	.0422	.0743	.0705	.0416	.0016
in Canada	(1.01)	(1.19)	(3.12)	(2.46)	(2.14)	(.01)

NOTE: The t-ratios are presented in parentheses.

types of persons emigrate the United States. Admittedly, native Americans leaving the U.S. may go to a number of alternative destinations. Even though no data exist on the number and/or destination of U.S. emigrants, it is reasonable to suppose that, due to geographical proximity, cultural similarity, and a shared language, Canada provides a relatively attractive destination for potential American emigrants, and that the sample of Americans living in Canada probably represents a large fraction of the population that has permanently left the United States. The analysis presented in this paper suggests that persons who left the United States (and went to Canada) in the post-1960 period have relatively poor labor market opportunities (in terms of unobservable skills). It was argued earlier that the average Canadian native and the average American native are quite similar in terms of skills and human capital. Under this assumption, the average American immigrant in Canada, by doing significantly worse than the average Canadian native, would also do significantly worse than the average American native. Hence the endogeneity of the migration decision leads to a negative selection of persons in the formation of the pool of emigrants to Canada.

The opposite is true when we consider the nature of the Canadian migrant flow to the United States. The latest wave of these individuals—even prior to any assimilation taking place—has already reached earnings parity with native Americans. Hence the selection mechanism generating this migration flow leads to a "brain drain" out of Canada and into the United States. In sum, therefore, the transnational labor flows are characterized by Canada exporting high-ability individuals and the United States exporting low-ability persons.

These results, of course, raise the important question of *why* the composition of transnational migration flows differs so radically between Canada and the United States. If it is assumed that these migration flows are motivated by wealth-maximizing behavior, it is possible to obtain some insights into the possible reasons for the observed selections. The wealth-maximizing model presented in chapter 3 shows that the only variable determining whether or not emigrants from any given country of origin are positively or negatively selected from the entire population is the *ratio* of the variance in the income distribution in the country of origin to the variance in the income distribution in the country of destination (assuming, as seems reasonable, that the correlation in earnings across the two countries is positive and sizable). If, for example, the United States has a more unequal income distribution than Canada, persons in the lower tail of the Canadian income distribution are "protected" from poor labor market outcomes and will do substantially worse if they were to migrate to the United States. On the other hand, persons in the upper tail of the Canadian income distribution are, in a sense, being heavily "taxed," and can find a substantial improvement in their wealth if they migrate to the United States. This model, therefore, predicts that migrants are positively selected when they migrate to countries that have more income inequality than the country of origin, and that migrants are negatively selected when they migrate to countries that have less income inequality than the country of origin.

The standard deviation of log earnings among natives in Canada is .5754, and the coefficient of variation of earnings (i.e., the ratio of the standard deviation to the arithmetic mean) is 1.227. On the other hand, the standard deviation of log earnings among native workers in the United States is .6219, and the coefficient of variation in earnings is 1.426. Earnings inequality, therefore, seems to be somewhat greater in the United States than in Canada. This fact alone, therefore, could generate the types of selection biases in the unmeasured skills of transnational migrants that have been documented in this paper.

Of course, differences in economic conditions and/or migration policies across the two countries also play a role in the determination of the composition of the transnational migration flows. The summary data describing the economies of Canada and the United States, however, show very little difference in both the level and the trends of key aggregate economic characteristics over the relevant period. Moreover, both Canadian and U.S. immigration policies are supposedly free of any national origin bias, and hence there is little reason to suspect that these policies alone could generate the differences in the composition of the migrant streams between the transnational migrants and immigrants from other countries. It is also worth noting that the skill-based Canadian immigration policy is, for the most part, restricting immigrants on the basis of observed skills. The analysis in this paper shows that sizable self-selection biases also exist in unobserved earning capacities, a parameter over which both the policy and immigration officials have little control. Thus the economic model of wealth-maximization provides the only consistent explanation of the selection mechanism guiding the transnational flows between Canada and the United States.

10

Summary and Conclusions

This monograph examines international differences in how immigrants perform in the labor market of their chosen country of residence. The main conceptual tool of the analysis is the insight that foreign-born persons in any given host country are not randomly drawn from the population of the various countries of origin. Two kinds of self-selection play a dominant role in the economics of immigration. First, there is selection in the determination of the composition of the pool of persons who leave any given country. This selection occurs both on the basis of observed socioeconomic characteristics (such as education) and in terms of unobserved individual characteristics (such as ability or productivity). In addition, this nonrandom sample of emigrants from any given country of origin is then sorted across various possible host countries in a nonrandom way. Hence the pool of foreign-born persons in any given host country is doubly self-selected: the pool of immigrants in the host country is composed of persons who found it profitable to leave the country of origin *and* who did not find it profitable to migrate anywhere else.

The insight that a nonrandom sorting of potential migrants and potential host countries occurs implies the existence of an "immigration market." In this marketplace, different countries "compete" for potential emigrants. This competition exists because different host countries offer potential migrants different sets of economic conditions (such as unemployment rates, income distributions, etc.), *and* different sets of migration policies (such as skill-based migration policies or policies based on the concept of family reunification). Potential migrants consider the benefits and costs associated with these economic and legal constraints, and sort themselves across the various host countries. The immigration market, therefore, plays the important role of allocating labor across international boundaries.

This monograph presents a theoretical and empirical analysis of the role played by the sorting of migrants and host countries in determining the labor market performance of foreign-born persons in the three largest host countries (Australia, Canada, and the United States). The theoretical analysis is based on the hypothesis that individuals choose their country of residence according to the principle of wealth-maximization. That is, given the institutional constraints, they move (or stay) in the country which provides them the highest earnings opportunities (net of migration costs).

The assumption of wealth-maximizing behavior provides important insights into the mechanics that guide the sorting that occurs in the immigration market. It was seen, for example, that the conditions required for positive (or negative) selection in observed characteristics (such as education) have *nothing* to do with the conditions required for positive (or negative) selection in unobserved abilities. In particular, the selection in terms of abilities is determined by comparisons of the extent of income distribution in the country of origin with the extent of income distribution in the country of destination. If the country of origin has more income inequality than the country of destination, the migration flow is negatively selected from the population in the country of origin. Conversely, if the country of origin has less income inequality than the country of destination, the migration flow is positively selected from the population in the country of origin.

The types of selection that occur in education, on the other hand, are based exclusively on a comparison of which country attaches a higher value to educational attainment. If the country of origin has a higher "rate of return" to education than the country of destination, highly educated individuals do not migrate. Conversely, if the country of origin has a lower rate of return to education than the country of destination, the migration flow is composed of highly-educated persons.

These results, therefore, suggest that it is entirely possible for a given country of destination to "import" highly-educated persons, but that these highly-educated persons are the least productive in the population of highly-educated persons in the country of origin. In other words, positive or negative selection in abilities can coexist with positive or negative selection in education. Little is learned, therefore, from comparisons of unstandardized wage levels between migrants and natives.

The empirical analysis reported in this monograph uses five census data sets from the three different host countries to document the labor market performance of foreign-born persons in Australia, Canada, and the United States. Among the major empirical findings of the study are:

1. There was a marked change in the types of migrants flowing to the host countries over the postwar period. Prior to the mid-1960s, the United States and Canada attracted migrants who performed quite well in the labor market (in terms of their earnings relative to those of comparable natives), while Australia attracted migrants who were not relatively successful in the Australian labor market. During the 1970s, however, a reversal in these rankings took place. Persons who now choose Australia as their destination perform very well in the Australian labor market, while those choosing the United States have very low earnings (as compared to natives in the U.S.).

2. About 80 percent of the variance in the relative earnings of the various cohorts of immigrants in each of the three host countries can be accounted for by a small set of variables describing a number of economic and institutional characteristics in the countries of origin and the countries of destination. For example, immigrants originating in countries with large per capita Gross National Products perform quite well in all three destination countries. In addition, immigrants originating in countries with high levels of income inequality have very low relative earnings in the host country, while persons migrating to host countries with high levels of income inequality perform very well in their chosen country of residence. It is noteworthy that these results are entirely consistent with the economic theory of immigration.

3. The changes in immigration policy initiated by the 1965 Amendments to the U.S. Immigration and Nationality Act induced a structural decline in the quality of immigrant cohorts that chose the U.S. as their destination. This law may be responsible for as much as a 5 percent

decline in the relative earnings of persons who migrated to the United States.

4. Persons who emigrate the United States differ substantially from the U.S.-born population that chooses to remain in the U.S. The study of American individuals who emigrated to Canada shows that these individuals have very low earnings despite their relatively high education level. American emigrants to Canada, therefore, are negatively selected (in terms of unobserved skill characteristics) from the population of American natives.

This brief list of substantive empirical findings shows the promise of this approach to the economics of immigration. Much of the modern literature analyzing the earnings of immigrants is quite myopic in its approach: the only relevant question seems to be how the earnings of immigrants compare to the earnings of natives in the country of destination. Economic theory suggests that much more can be learned about the selection process if immigrants are also compared to "stayers" (i.e., persons from the same country of origin that chose not to migrate) and if immigrants in any given host country are compared to migrants who chose other host countries as their destination. This monograph shows that the joint analysis of census data sets from different host countries leads to useful insights into the types of selections that characterize the immigrant population and into the workings of the immigration market. Future research along these lines, therefore, is likely to substantially increase our understanding of the immigration experience.

BIBLIOGRAPHY

Australian Department of Immigration and Ethnic Affairs, *Australian Immigration, 1788–1978,* Australian Government Printing Office, 1978.

Beggs, John J. and Bruce J. Chapman. "Immigrant Wage and Unemployment Experience in Australia," Mimeograph, September 1987.

Birrell, R. "A New Era in Australian Migration Policy," *International Migration Review,* Spring 1984.

Bloom, David E. and Morley K. Gunderson. "Canadian Immigration," Mimeograph, September 1987.

Borjas, George J. "The Earnings of Male Hispanic Immigrants in the United States," *Industrial and Labor Relations Review,* April 1982.

––––. "Assimilation, Changes in Cohort Quality, and the Earnings of Immigrants," *Journal of Labor Economics,* October 1985.

––––. "Self-Selection and the Earnings of Immigrants," *American Economic Review,* September 1987 (a).

––––. "Immigration and Self-Selection," October 1987 (b).

Borjas, George J. and Marta Tienda. "The Economic Consequences of Immigration," *Science,* February 6, 1987.

Boyd, Monica. "Immigration Policies and Trends: A Comparison of Canada and the United States," *Demography,* February 1976.

Canada, Department of Employment and Immigration. *Immigration Statistics,* various issues.

Canada, Department of Employment and Immigration. *Annual Report,* various issues.

Canada Statistics. *Historical Statistics of Canada,* various issues.

Canada Statistics. *Canada Yearbook,* various issues.

Carliner, Geoffrey. "Wages, Earnings, and Hours of Work of First,

Second, and Third Generation American Males," *Economic Inquiry*, January 1980.

Chiswick, Barry R. "The Effect of Americanization on the Earnings of Foreign-Born Men," *Journal of Political Economy*, October 1978.

_____. "Immigration Policies, Source Countries, and Immigrant Skills," Mimeograph, 1987.

Chiswick, Barry R. and Paul Miller. "Immigrant Generation and Income in Australia," *Economic Record*, 1985.

DeFreitas, Gregory. "The Earnings of Immigrants in the American Labor Market." Ph.D. Dissertation, Columbia University, 1980.

Douglas, Paul H. "Is the New Immigration More Unskilled than the Old?" *Journal of the American Statistical Association*, June 1919.

Greenwood, Michael J. "Research on Internal Migration in the United States: A Survey," *Journal of Economic Literature*, June 1975.

Greenwood, Michael J. and John M. McDowell. "The Factor Market Consequences of Immigration," *Journal of Economic Literature*, December 1986.

Heckman, James J. "Sample Selection Bias as a Specification Error," *Econometrica*, January 1979.

Heckman, James J. and Richard Robb. "Using Longitudinal Data to Estimate Age, Period, and Cohort Effects in Earnings Equations," in H. Winsborough and O. Duncan, eds., *Analyzing Longitudinal Data for Age, Period, and Cohort Effects*. New York: Academic Press, 1983.

Hicks, John R. *The Theory of Wages*, Second Edition. New York: St. Martin's Press, 1966.

Jasso, Guillermina and Mark Rosenzweig. "How Well Do U.S. Immigrants Do? Vintage Effects, Emigration Selectivity, and the Occupational Mobility of Immigrants," Mimeograph, 1985.

_____ and _____. "Family Reunification and the Immigration Multiplier: U.S. Immigration Law, Origin-Country Conditions, and the Reproduction of Immigrants," *Demography*, August 1986.

Keely, Charles B. "The United States of America," in D. Kubat, ed.,

The Politics of Migration Policies. New York: Center for Migration Studies, 1979.

Keely, Charles B. and Patricia Elwell, "International Migration: The United States and Canada," in M. Kritz and S. Tomasi, eds., *Global Trends in Migration*. New York: Center for Migration Studies, 1981.

Kubat, Daniel. "Canada," in *The Politics of Migration Policies*. New York: Center for Migration Studies, 1979.

Lavoie, Yolande. *L'Emigration des Canadiens aux Etats-Unis avant 1930*. Montreal: Universite de Montreal, 1972.

Long, James E. "The Effect of Americanization on Earnings: Some Evidence for Women," *Journal of Political Economy*, June 1980.

Lydall, Harold. *The Structure of Earnings*. New York: Oxford University Press, 1968.

Price, Charles. "Australia," in D. Kubat, ed., *The Politics of Migration Policies*. New York: Center for Migration Studies, 1979.

Roy, Andrew D. "Some Thoughts on the Distribution of Earnings," *Oxford Economic Papers*, June 1951.

Schwartz, Aba. "Migration and Lifetime Earnings in the U.S." Ph.D. Dissertation, University of Chicago, 1968.

Sjaastad, Larry A. "The Costs and Returns of Human Migration," *Journal of Political Economy*, October 1962 Supplement.

Tandon, B.B. "Earnings Differentials Among Native Born and Foreign Born Residents of Canada," *International Migration Review*, Fall 1978.

United Nations. *Demographic Indicators of Countries*. New York: United Nations, 1982.

U.S. Department of Commerce. *Statistical Abstract of the United States*, various issues.

U.S. Immigration and Naturalization Service. *Statistical Yearbook of the Immigration and Naturalization Service*, U.S. Government Printing Office, various issues.

Zolberg, Aristide R. "Contemporary Transnational Migrations in Historical Perspective: Patterns and Dilemmas," in M. Kritz, ed., *U.S. Immigration and Refugee Policy.* Lexington, MA: Lexington Books, 1983.

Zubrzycki, Jerzy. "International Migration in Australasia and the South Pacific," in M. Kritz and S. Tomasi, eds., *Global Trends in Migration.* New York: Center for Migration Studies, 1981.

INDEX

African immigrants, 44, 45
Age: as factor determining earnings, 35-39; *See also* Cohorts
American immigrants: performance in Canadian labor market, 78-92
Asian immigrants, 12, 45
Assimilation: rate among Canadian and American migrants of, 89-90; rate of, 35, 52, 61-62, 64, 65
Australia: Asian immigrants in, 45; calculation of entry-level wages for immigrants in, 65; effect of education on earnings in, 47, 48; immigrant earnings in, 50, 52, 53; immigration policy in, 14-16; native-born in, 44, 55-56, 64-66, 68, 72; qualiity of immigrants in, 53, 66-67; size and composition of immigrant pool, 16; White Australia Policy in, 15

Beggs, John J., 4
Birrell, R., 16
Bloom, David E., 4, 61
Borjas, George J., 3, 4, 7n2, 8n2, 28, 32n1, 32n2, 32n3, 39n1, 52, 57
Boyd, Monica, 17n1, 79
British immigrants: performance in Canadian and U.S. labor markets, 85-88

Canada: change in composition of immigrants and migrant flow, 53-54, 59; decline in immigrant earnings, 61; immigration policy in, 12-14, 93; native-born in, 55-56, 57-64; percent of foreign-born persons in, 79-80; performance of American immigrants in, 79-93; performance of immigrants in, 44, 45, 53-54, 59; rate of assimilation of immigrants in, 61-65; *See also* Immigration Act of 1962 (Canada)
Canadian immigrants: entry wage differential for, 88; performance in labor market, 82-85; performance in U.S. labor market, 78-92
Carliner, Geoffrey, 8n3
Chapman, Bruce J., 4
Chiswick, Barry R., 8n3
Cohorts: analysis to determine wage differential between foreign- and native-born, 4, 50-72; changes for U.S. and Canada in quality of, 60-61, 85; position as factor determining earnings in, 35-39
Country of destination. *See* Host country
Country-of-origin emigrants: basis of selection for, 95; differences in destination of, 5-7; effect of income inequality on decision to emigrate, 73-76; role of GNP to determine quality of, 74-75
Country-of-origin immigrants: change in composition in Canada of, 14, 53-54, 59-60; change in composition in United States of, 60

Data sources, 41-42
Defreitas, Gregory, 8n3
Douglas, Paul H., 23

Earnings, immigrant: in Australia, 44; in Canada, 44, 53, 57-58, 60-61; early and current analyses of, 2-5; effect of country income inequality on, 76; empirical evidence for, 35-39; factors determining, 35-37; growth rates of, 38-39; in host country, 2-3; impact of socioeconomic variables on, 48-49; reasons for decline in Canada and U.S., 60; relative, 74, 79-80, 97; *See also* Quality; Wage, entry level

Earnings, native. *See* Native-born persons
Earnings distribution: analysis of, 20-21
Earnings functions: analysis of, 29-30, 47-52, 84-89; *See also* Wealth maximization
Economic conditions: effect on migration of, 28-29; as factor determining earnings, 35-39
Education: effect on earnings in Australia, 48; value to labor markets of, 47, 48, 82-85, 96
Elwell, Patricia, 17n1
Emigrants: performance of Canadian, 79-93; performance of U.S. 79-98; selection process and characteristics of, 19; self-selection by, 95; sorting by immigration market of pool of, 68
Europeans: relative earnings as immigrants, 44-45, 53, 59

Family reunification concept: under 1965 amendments to U.S. immigration laws, 10-11, 12; in Australia, 16; in Canadian law, 13; effect on quality of migrant pool of, 28
Foreign-born persons: differences in characteristics of, 19; effect of U.S. post-1965 immigration policy on, 11; equations to measure life-cycle wealth of, 37-39; as percent of population in Canada and U.S., 79-80; as percent of population in host countries of, 1; *See also* Migrant flow; Migrant pool

GNP (Gross National Product), per capita: as variable to qualify labor market performance, 74-75
Greenwood, Michael J., 8n3, 22
Growth rate: of immigrant and native workers, 37-39, 66
Gunderson, Morley K., 4, 61

Heckman, James J., 24, 36
Hicks, John R., 22
Host country: choices of high ability workers, 24-25; effect of income inequality on immigrant performance, 73-76; effect of unemployment rate on immigrant earnings, 75; *See also* Australia; Canada; United States

Immigrant pool. *See* Migrant pool
Immigrants: analysis and definition of quality of, 73; assimilation rate of Africans and Asians, 62; changes in country of origin, 11-12, 13-14; changes in earnings expectations for U.S., 57; comparison across countries studied of, 45; effect of socioeconomic variables on earnings of, 48-49; *See also* Foreign-born persons
Immigration Act of 1962 (Canada): effect of, 12; effect of 1976 amendments, 13-14
Immigration and Nationality Act (United States): effect of 1965 and subsequent amendments to, 10-12, 27-28, 97-98; pre-1965 legislation under, 9-10, 27
Immigration market: description of, 5, 19; effect of classification (sorting) by, 73-77; evidence for existence and role of, 7, 95-96; example of actions of, 78-92; pool in Australia for, 16; role of, 45, 68-69; shift in U.S. competitiveness in, 72; *See also* Immigrants; Migrant pool; Quality; Self-selection; Sorting
Immigration policy: in Australia, 14-16; in Canada, 12-14, 93; as determinant of quality of migration flows, 28-29, 73, 76; effect of, 28; effect of changes in U.S., 72, 76-77, 83, 97-98; effect of restrictions on migrants, 9-10, 15-16; in host countries, 9-16; *See also* Canada; Immigration Act of 1962 (Canada); Immigration and Nationality Act (United States); United States

Income inequality: effect in country of origin and host country of, 24-27, 73, 75-76
Income-maximization hypothesis. *See* Wealth-maximization hypothesis

Jasso, Guillermina, 4, 17n3

Keely, Charles B., 17n1
Kinship regulations. *See* Family reunification concept
Kubat, Daniel, 13, 17n1

Latin American immigrants: earnings in Canada, 55; earnings in U.S. labor market, 53
Lavoie, Yolande, 79
Life-cycle wealth: analysis and comparison of foreign- and native-born persons, 37-39, 68; measurement of, 66
Long, James E., 8n3
Low ability workers: choice of host country, 25-26
Lydall, Harold, 21

McDowell, John M., 8n3
Migrant flow: between Canada and U.S., 79-93; change in Canada of, 59; labor market performance of, 73-77; model as predictor of factors determining size of, 22; observed skill characteristics of, 29; size and composition of, 1, 5, 16, 28, 77, 97
Migrant pool: analyses of, 24-27; decline in quality of, 60-61; factors influencing change in composition of, 28-29; quality in Australia of, 52, 53; quality in U.S. of, 27, 28, 52; quality of, 26, 37, 52; self-selection by, 45; unobserved skill characteristics in, 20-26; *See also* Selection conditions; Self-selection
Migration: country income equality as incentive for, 76; factor of return, 20; factors influencing decision for, 9-16, 22
Miller, Paul, 8n3

National origin. *See* Country of origin
Native-born persons: effect of socioeconomic variables on earnings of, 48-49; measurement of life-cycle wealth of, 37-39, 66, 68; ratio in Canada and U.S. of foreign-born to, 79-80; relative earnings in Australia and Canada for, 44; *See also* Australia; Canada; United States

Performance, labor market: comparison of Canadian and U.S. emigrants and native-born, 79-93; country-of-origin groups, 72; determinants of emigrant and immigrant, 73-77; of foreign-born in host country, 7, 68; GNP as variable to identify, 74-75; success of ethnic or national origin groups in, 45-46; transnational migrant and British immigrant differential, 88; *See also* Earnings, immigrant
Period effects: as factor in determining earnings, 35, 36, 49
Point system: in Australia, 16; in Canada, 13
Present value differentials, 66-68, 74; *See also* Life-cycle wealth
Price, Charles, 15, 17n1

Quality: of immigrants, 73; of migrants, 23, 27, 37; *See also* Selection conditions; Self-selection
Quota system: effect of post-1965 redistribution in U.S. of, 11, 27; pre-1965 in U.S., 9-10, 27; *See also* Immigration policy

Refugee populations: characteristics of, 26-27
Return migration. *See* Migration
Robb, Richard, 36
Rosenzweig, Mark, 4, 17n3
Roy, Andrew D., 19

Schwartz, Aba, 84
Selection conditions: observed and unobserved, 23-24, 96; for observed migrant characteristics, 29-32; for unobserved migrant characteristics, 20-27, 31-32
Selectivity bias, 24, 30
Self-selection: factors influencing, 24-26, 31-32; by host countries of foreign-born immigrants, 19, 45-46, 69, 95; in migrant pool, 95; migration from high and low income inequality countries, 76; *See also* Selection conditions
Sjaastad, Larry A., 22
Skills, immigrant: as factor determining quality, 73; incentives to migrate, 76; quality of, 85
Sorting: factors; of immigrants by immigration market, 19, 52, 73-77; of refugees by immigration market, 26-27; *See also* Self-selection

Tandon, B. B., 8n3
Tienda, Maria, 7n2

Unemployment rate: effect in host country of, 75
United States: decline in earnings expectations for immigrants to, 57; decline in immigrant earnings, 61; earnings of African, Asian and European immigrants in, 44, 45; effect of change in immigrant composition, 44; effect of immigrant policy in, 9-12, 76-77; native-born in, 57-64; percent of foreign-born persons in, 79-80; performance of Canadian immigrants in, 79-93; quality of migrants to, 27-28, 52, 76-77; rate of assimilation in, 61-65; shift in competitiveness in immigration market of, 72, 77; *See also* Immigrants; Immigration and Nationality Act (United States); Immigration policy; Quota system

Value differentials: among countries studied, 66
Visa allocation (United States): post-1965 change in, 27-28

Wage, entry level; in Australia, Canada and United States, 63-67; correlation with assimilation rates, 64-66; as criterion for quality of immigrant, 37-39
Wage differentials, 50-54, 64, 86-89; *See also* Earnings, immigrant
Wealth-maximiation hypothesis, 7, 21-22, 27, 29, 76, 84, 92, 93, 96
White Australia Policy: effect and abolition of, 15-16

Zolberg, Aristide R., 8n2